MIAMI
THEN & NOW

MIAMI
THEN & NOW

ARVA MOORE PARKS & CAROLYN KLEPSER

THUNDER BAY
P·R·E·S·S

San Diego, California

Thunder Bay Press
An imprint of the Advantage Publishers Group
5880 Oberlin Drive, San Diego, CA 92121-4794
www.thunderbaybooks.com

Produced by PRC Publishing Ltd,
64 Brewery Road, London N7 9NT, England

A member of **Chrysalis** Books plc

© 2002 PRC Publishing Ltd.

All notations of errors or omissions should be addressed to Thunder Bay Press,
editorial department, at the above address. All other correspondence (author inquiries,
permissions, and rights) concerning the content of this book should be addressed to
PRC Publishing Ltd, 64 Brewery Road, London N7 9NT, England.

Library of Congress Cataloging-in-Publication Data
Parks, Arva Moore, 1939–
Miami then & now / Arva Moore Parks & Carolyn Klepser. pcm.
ISBN 1-57145-852-2
1. Miami (Fla.) -- History--Pictorial Works. 2. Miami (Fla.) -- Pictorial works.
I. Title: Miami then and now. II. Klepser, Carolyn. III. Title.
F319.M6.P373 2002
975.9'381'002--dc21   2002028924

Printed in Taiwan
1 2 3 4 5 06 05 04 03 02

ACKNOWLEDGMENTS:
The authors wish to thank everyone who helped with this book, particularly the following: Sam
Boldrick at the Miami-Dade Public Library, Steve Bovo at Hialeah Race Course, Carrollton School,
Steve Chatelaine at the Surf Club, Regina Dodd, Kathleen Dorkowski at Mount Sinai Medical Center,
Julio Grabiel at Spillis Candela, The Grafton Family, Sheila Hellman, Argelio Hernandez at Miami-
Dade County, Dawn Hugh at the Historical Museum of Southern Florida, Megan Kelly at Swire
Properties, The Mandarin Oriental, Hank Morrison, Robert Parcher at the City of Miami Beach, Laura
Pincus, Ransom Everglades School, Anuca Valverde, Nellie Vega for the Fisher Island Club, and James
P. Wendler.

PHOTO CREDITS:
The publisher wishes to thank the following for kindly supplying the "then" photographs for
this book:

Pages 6 and 8, Ralph M. Munroe Collection, Historical Museum of Southern Florida;
Pages 10, 14, and 16, Thelma Peters Collection, Arva Parks & Company;
Pages 12, 20, 24, 26, 34, 36, 40, 42, 54, 58, 66, 102, 110, 112 (inset, top), 122, and 132, Arva
Parks & Company;
Page 18, Daley Highleyman Collection, Arva Parks & Company;
Page 22, Black Archives;
Pages 28, 32, 62, 72, 74, 76, 78, 80, 106, and 116 (right), State of Florida Photographic
Archives;
Pages 30, 92, 94, 114, 116 (left), 126, 134, and 136, Matlack Collection, Historical Museum of
Southern Florida;
Pages 38, 70, 82, and 84, Miami News Collection, Arva Parks & Company;
Pages 44, 46, and 142, City of Miami;
Pages 48 and 56, Patty Catlow Collection, Arva Parks & Company;
Page 50, Kate Stirrup Dean Collection, Arva Parks & Company;
Page 52, Merrick Collection, Arva Parks & Company;
Page 60, Alice Wood Collection, Arva Parks & Company;
Pages 64, 86, 88, 90, and 140, Romer Collection, Miami-Dade Public Library;
Page 68, Don Kuhn Collection, Arva Parks & Company;
Pages 96, LeGro Collection, Historical Museum of Southern Florida;
Pages 98 and 112 (main picture), photographs by Claude Matlack, for Mr. Thomas J. Pancoast,
Miami Beach (now in the collection of Marty Pancoast Grafton);
Pages 100 and 124, City Clerk's Archive, City of Miami Beach;
Page 104 supplied courtesy of the Fisher Island Club;
Page 108, Pete Chase Collection, Arva Parks & Company;
Page 118, Jay Spence Collection, Historical Museum of Southern Florida;
Page 120, Mary McIsaacs Collection, Historical Museum of Southern Florida;
Pages 128 and 130, Wendler Collection, State of Florida Photographic Archives;
Page 138, Curt Teich Postcard Archives, Lake County Discovery Museum, Wauconda, Illinois.

Thanks to Simon Clay for taking all the "now" photography in this book, with the exception
of the photographs on the following pages:
Pages 11, 21, 23, 67, and 85 (inset, top), courtesy of Arva Moore Parks;
Page 13 kindly supplied by Swire Properties;
Pages 15 and 119, courtesy of Carolyn Klepser;
Page 37, courtesy of Argelio Hernandez, Miami-Dade County;
Page 81, courtesy of © Dan Forer;
Page 101, kindly supplied by the Mount Sinai Medical Center;
Page 103, kindly supplied by the Fontainebleau Hilton.

Front and back covers show the Miami River in the 1940s (photo: City of Miami, via Arva
Parks & Company) and today (photo: Simon Clay). See pages 46 and 47 for further details.
Front flap photographs show Miracle Mile in Coral Gables, then (photo, top: Miami News, via
Arva Parks & Company) and as it looks today (photo, bottom: Simon Clay). See pages 84 and
85 for further details.
Back flap photographs show Flagler Street looking east, in c.1922 (photo, top: Arva Parks &
Company) and today (photo, bottom: Simon Clay). See pages 26 and 27 for further details.
Page 1 shows Miami Beach, then (photo: © Bettmann/CORBIS).
Page 2 shows: Miami Beach as it looks today (photo: © Buddy Mays/CORBIS).

INTRODUCTION

"From all sorts and kinds of reasons we have come here, but we stay because we believe tremendously in this place and its future."

Marjory Stoneman Douglas, 1922

No other place is like Miami. It's the nation's youngest major city and its only subtropical megalopolis. Vibrant, alive, and constantly changing, the city attracts all kinds of people. The first arrived more than 10,000 years ago and built settlements on the bay and on a river they called Mayami. The land was theirs for thousands of years until the Spanish sailed in and claimed it for themselves. Bahamian seamen, adept at salvaging the remains of ships that crashed upon the Great Florida Reef, left their island homes and made new ones in South Florida. The Seminole tribe fled the white man's advancing civilization and arrived in Florida, determined to stay. After the United States acquired Florida from Spain in 1821, U.S. soldiers tried and failed to dislodge them from their Everglades home.

Without roads or even trails, the future City of Miami was a nameless, barely inhabited, and mostly unwanted terra incognita when Julia Tuttle arrived from Cleveland in 1891 to claim her 640-acre purchase on the north bank of the Miami River. Her nearest neighbors, William and Mary Brickell, ran a trading post on the other side of the river. They had been there for twenty years and owned more than 2,500 acres of undeveloped land. A few other brave pioneers lived on a scattering of barely improved homesteads and in three small settlements—Coconut Grove, Lemon City, and Cutler. Across the bay, only the House of Refuge, a government life-saving station for shipwrecked sailors, stood sentinel over a failed coconut plantation.

While most saw only an inhospitable, impenetrable, mosquito-infested jungle, Julia Tuttle predicted that the area's geography guaranteed it would someday become a great international city. With a pledge of frost-free winters, half her land, and a promise of more from the Brickells, she convinced Henry Flagler to extend his railroad to Miami, lay out a town, and build a luxury hotel. The first train arrived in April 1896 and by July, 344 men, a third of whom were black, incorporated the instant "Magic City" of Miami.

In the early years of the twentieth century, Miami lost its raw, frontier atmosphere. It began to take on the appearance of a respectable small town that each winter transformed itself into a lively tourist haven. Besides the tourists, Miami also attracted northern industrialists who turned the Brickells' grand new avenue into a "Millionaires' Row." James Deering, a farm machinery magnate, built the beautiful Villa Vizcaya on 180 acres of bayfront land and launched an architectural style that remains popular today.

Carl Fisher, another Brickell Avenue millionaire, invested in a half-finished causeway that connected John Collins's avocado-growing enterprise to the mainland. As part of the deal, Collins transferred a large swath of beach real estate to Fisher. In 1915, Miami Beach became the second South Florida city created to please the tourists.

By all normal standards, Miami was a perpetual boomtown. In the 1920s, the word boom even became a proper noun. The Florida Boom even rivaled the 1849 California Gold Rush for national attention. Almost overnight, the city quadrupled its population, changed its skyline, and exploded its borders.

Of the many legendary developers, George Merrick was in a class by himself. He created Coral Gables—South Florida's first totally planned community. It had a Spanish/Mediterranean theme, complete with beautiful entrances, plazas, and wide boulevards. Phenomenally successful, the development further boosted the popularity of Miami.

Other developers joined in the frenzy and created a variety of fantasy subdivisions, each with a different architectural theme. Not to be outdone, Carl Fisher built luxurious hotels on Miami Beach, as well as other amenities like polo fields and golf courses to please his ever-increasing cadre of millionaire visitors and residents. For a while, it seemed that the Boom would last forever—until nature accelerated the inevitable bust with a killer hurricane. After the September 17–18, 1926, disaster, northern headlines proclaimed: "Miami is Wiped Out." It was barely an exaggeration.

By the time the 1929 stock market crash plunged the nation into depression, Miami and Miami Beach had already suffered three years of economic ruin. By the mid-1930s, however, while the rest of the nation continued to wallow, more than one hundred new hotels and apartment buildings with stark Moderne lines began to rise on Miami Beach. Although no one knew it at the time, these buildings would not only lead Miami out of depression, they would also become the heart of the world-famous Art Deco District that sixty years later would bring the area international fame.

During World War II, the U.S. Army Air Force took over most of Miami Beach's hotels and apartments and the Navy moved into Miami. Fisher's and Merrick's glamorous hotels became hospitals, posh golf courses became drill fields, and ritzy clubs became mess halls.

After the war, Miami boomed again when thousands of veterans returned to start new lives under the warm sun. Growth continued unabated into the 1950s. Miami Beach welcomed a string of glitzy new luxury hotels and kitschy motels. Miami spread out in all directions.

When Fidel Castro took over Cuba in 1959, no one had any idea that the Castro revolution would change Miami as much as it would Cuba. During the next twenty years, more than half a million Cubans came to South Florida. At first they flocked to an older Miami neighborhood called Riverside, changing it into a vibrant "Little Havana." From this launching place, the Cubans ultimately transformed Miami into the great international city that Julia Tuttle predicted. Other refugees from Latin America and the Caribbean sought out Miami's hospitable shores, adding their own special magic to what was becoming an increasingly cosmopolitan city of constantly changing faces.

Today Miami is thriving on change. The skyline is once again filled with construction cranes as another new Miami emerges and another "now" turns into a "then." No longer at the end of something, Miami is at the middle of everything—the connector of the Americas and the center of an exciting new world.

Arva Moore Parks

In 1884, Ralph M. Munroe, South Florida's first photographer, shot this earliest known photograph of Miami's oldest structure. Built on Key Biscayne in 1825, the Seminole tribe attacked and burned it in 1836. The structure was rebuilt in 1847, with an additional twenty-six feet added in 1855. Confederate guerillas destroyed the lens during the Civil War and the beacon remained dark until 1867. When the Fowey Rock light went into service in 1878, the Cape Florida light was extinguished.

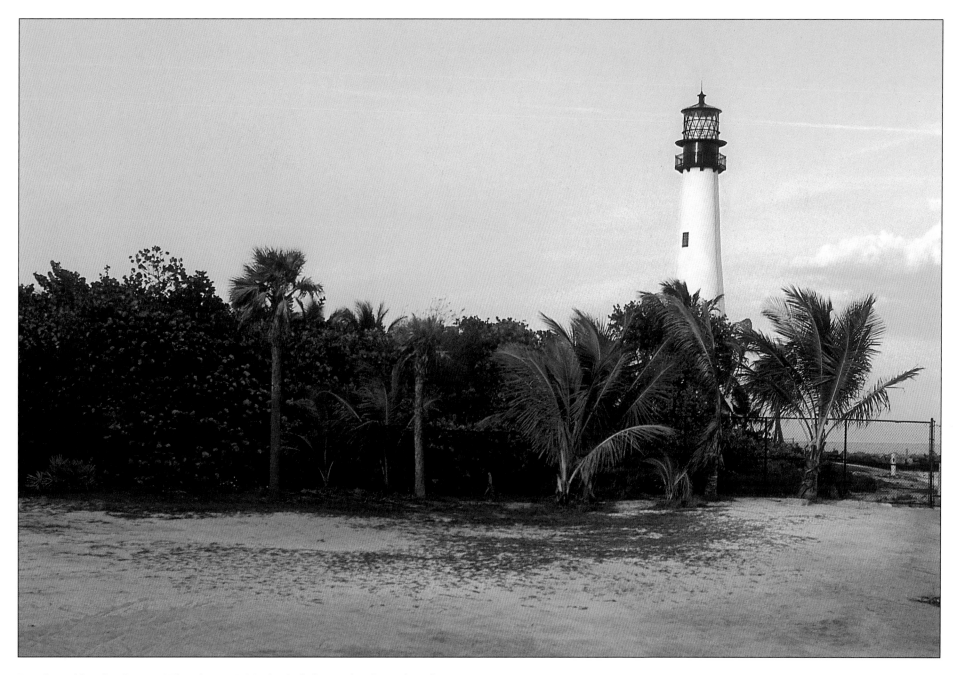

Purchased by the State of Florida in 1966, the lighthouse has been listed on the National Register of Historic Places since 1971. In 1988, Dade Heritage Trust, Miami-Dade County's preservation organization, began a grassroots movement to completely restore the deteriorating structure. Completed in 1996, its public reopening coincided with Miami's Centennial Celebration. Today it is the focal point of Bill Baggs Cape Florida State Park.

When Ralph M. Munroe took this photograph in the 1880s, the long building on the left served as a trading post and the Dade County Courthouse. South Carolinian William F. English built both structures in the 1840s at the conclusion of the Second Seminole War. When renewed hostilities with the Seminoles forced him to abandon his property, the U.S. Army returned, reactivated Fort Dallas, and completed the two stone buildings for their own use.

In 1925, the Miami Women's Club and the Daughters of the American
Revolution launched Miami's first preservation effort to save what was known
as Fort Dallas. They moved the building upriver to the City of Miami's
Lummus Park, where it remains today. Although it served as part of Fort
Dallas from 1849–57, its first use was as quarters for William English's slaves.
It is also Miami's first "coral rock" building.

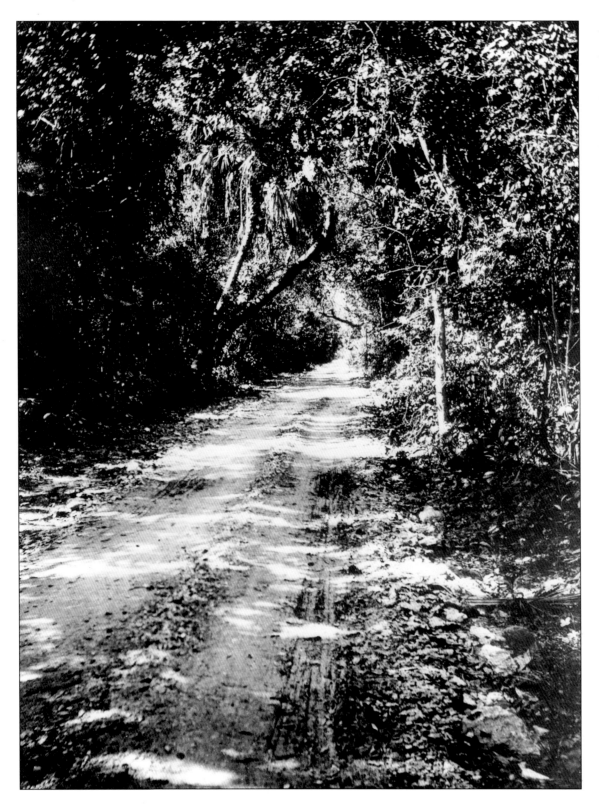

Left: A dense, tropical hardwood forest covered much of the land that would become downtown Miami. After William and Mary Brickell purchased more than 2,000 acres on the south side of the Miami River in 1871, people called the tangled jungle the "Brickell Hammock." This 1890s view shows the Coconut Grove Trail that linked the pioneer community to the Miami River. In the future, this pathway would become Brickell Avenue.

Right: Brickell Avenue is Miami's most glamorous commercial street. While Henry Flagler platted narrow streets on his side of the river, William and Mary Brickell had a bolder vision. They built this beautiful boulevard in 1911 and turned it into Miami's first "Millionaires' Row." Rezoned for high-rise buildings in the 1950s, the homes have been replaced with modern skyscrapers. A monument to Mary Brickell can be seen on the median.

In January 1897, Henry Flagler's grand Royal Palm Hotel opened. It was a huge "Flagler Yellow" mansard roofed building—five stories tall and almost 700 feet long. Its twinkling electric lights—Miami's first—made it stand out as a veritable fairyland in the midst of the raw, infant city. Damaged by the 1926 hurricane, it was torn down in 1930 and the site became a parking lot.

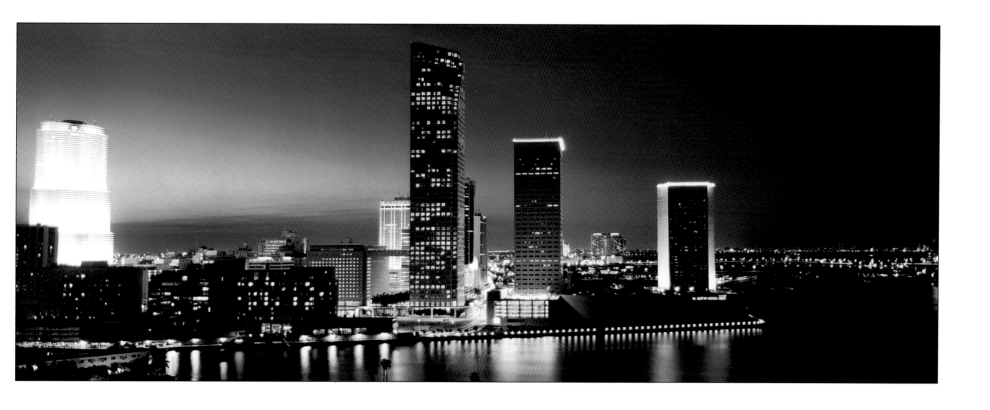

At night, the Magic City lives up to its name. Lofty towers radiate a palette of glimmering colors. With the wave of a wand, the Bank of America Tower (left), designed by I.M. Pei, changes its evening glow to match the season. Not to be outdone, the honeycombed luminescence of the First Union Financial Center—Miami's tallest office building (center)—casts its nightly spell across the bay.

Miami's first grammar school, seen here, opened in 1897. In 1911, the school board built a new concrete building that housed grades one through twelve. A hotelier purchased the old wooden school, moved it to Third Street and Miami Avenue, and transformed it into the Frances Hotel. The federal government acquired the school property in 1931 and tore down the 1911 building to clear the site for a new Federal Courthouse and Central Post Office.

The old Federal Courthouse and former Central Post Office has been called "A Monument to Three Artists"—Phineas Paist, Harold D. Stewart, and Denman Fink. The neoclassical design is influenced by the Mediterranean Revival style made famous by Paist and Fink in Coral Gables. Dedicated on July 1, 1933, its walls are clad in limestone. The tall buildings are the James Lawrence King Federal Justice Building and the Federal Detention Center.

Left: In 1905, Canadians Salem and Emily Graham built the Halcyon Hotel from locally quarried oolitic limestone. For years, people mistakenly believed that Stanford White, the legendary New York architect, designed the building. Mrs. Graham reportedly said that he only did a quick rendering of the facade on the back of an envelope. In 1937, after years of ups and downs, the DuPont National Bank Corporation bought the property and demolished the hotel.

Right: Sometimes called "Miami's Rockefeller Center," the Alfred I. DuPont Building, designed by the Jacksonville architectural firm Marsh and Saxelbye, opened with great fanfare in October 1939. Nearly 35,000 Miamians passed through the doors of the notable Depression Moderne building on opening day and ogled the impressive, brass bas-relief elevator doors and the lavishly decorated ceilings.

In 1911, Locke T. Highleyman developed Point View, one of Miami's first exclusive neighborhoods. He was the first to dredge up the bay bottom to create new land from mangroves. Local luminaries like Frank Shutts, owner of *The Miami Herald*, and millionaire winter residents like William H. Luden, of cough drop fame, built impressive mansions on what is today Brickell Bay Drive—still one of Miami's most beautiful streets.

Today all the mansions are gone and the bayfront is filled with luxury high-rise apartments, hotels, and condominiums. Zoning and lifestyle changes doomed the large estates and elegant homes. One by one, they came down and new owners built modern skyscrapers in their place. When completed, the Four Seasons Hotel and Tower (right background) will be the tallest residential building south of New York.

In 1916, Margaret Burlingame purchased a five-acre spoil bank and named it Burlingame Island. The island was barely visible to anyone except the Brickells, who lived across the river from Henry Flagler's Royal Palm Hotel (right). For decades, little changed on the scraggy spit of land except its size. When Edward N. Claughton purchased it in 1943 and renamed it Claughton Island, it had grown to twenty acres.

In the late 1970s, Hong Kong–based Swire Properties purchased most of the island, renamed it Brickell Key, and created a master plan that led to the creation of today's unique island community of more than 1,000 residential units and 340,000 square feet of office and retail space. The addition of the five-star Mandarin Oriental Hotel in November 2000 added to the glamour of what has been billed as "America's only downtown island resort."

In 1896, Julia Tuttle and Henry Flagler laid out "Colored Town," west of the railroad tracks between today's Northwest Sixth and Twelfth Streets. Its bustling Avenue G, seen here in this c. 1915 view, had professional offices, more than thirty stores, and the Lyric Theater (the building with the cupola). Built by Geder Walker in 1913, writers called the Lyric "the most beautiful and costly playhouse owned by colored people in all the Southland."

The restored Lyric Theater is the centerpiece of the Historic Folklife Village in the section now known as Overtown/Park West. Led by Black Archives founder Dorothy Jenkins Fields, future plans include further development of the Folklife Village and the revival of the neighborhood as "Little Broadway," its 1930s–60s' nickname when it was a popular tourist destination and entertainment and cultural center.

The Miami City Hospital, designed by August Geiger, opened in 1918, just in time for the terrible flu epidemic. Criticized for being "way out in the country," doctors passed a motion asking the administration to fence in the area to keep cows from grazing under the operating room windows. In 1924, soon after the death of beloved pioneer doctor James M. Jackson, the City Commission changed the hospital's name to Jackson Memorial Hospital.

Today's Jackson Memorial Hospital, one of the busiest in the nation, is a county-owned hospital and major teaching facility for the University of Miami School of Medicine. The campus also includes such stellar institutions as the Bascom Palmer Eye Institute and the Sylvester Comprehensive Cancer Center. The old hospital, known as "the Alamo," was saved from the wrecking ball in 1977 and moved a short distance to become the centerpiece of the new complex.

When this photograph was taken c. 1922, the impressive new First National Bank Building (left), Miami's tallest and most elegant skyscraper to date, was almost completed. The multiturreted Halcyon Hotel dominated the other end of the block that was filled with an assortment of real estate offices, banks, stores, and no fewer than four shopping arcades. In the distance, Elser Pier's new electric sign announced the popular entertainment venue.

The old First National Bank Building still stands, although it suffers from an insensitive 1960s remodeling. The Alfred I. DuPont Building, that replaced the Halcyon Hotel, marks the end of the block. Elser Pier is long gone, torn down in the 1920s when the bay bottom was pumped up to create Bayfront Park. Currently undergoing beautification, Flagler Street sports new streetlights reminiscent of the classic 1920s style.

Left: In this June 1926 photograph, a Coral Gables Rapid Transit car prepares to turn at SE First Avenue. The Seminole and McCrory Hotels, with their tourist-friendly balconies (right), remained as reminders of the Magic City's earlier days. In the distance, the Bank of Biscayne Bay Building added a new silhouette to the constantly changing skyline. Behind it, the skeleton of the ziggurat-topped Miami-Dade County Courthouse, then under construction, is visible.

Right: With the exception of the 1950s Morris Lapidus–designed Ainsley Building (right), this section of today's Flagler Street looks remarkably like it did in 1926. Although the former hotels have a new facade and have lost their balconies, the distinctive roofline remains. Some of the 1920s details survive near the pinnacle of the Biscayne Building, and the peak of the Miami-Dade County Courthouse is still visible just behind it.

Left: The Scottish Rite Masonic Temple, designed by the prominent architectural firm of Kiehnel and Elliott, was dedicated on March 12, 1924. Built at the start of the King Tut Egyptian Revival craze, the unique structure is also Miami's first Art Deco building. During the Depression, it housed the WPA's Federal Theater and became an Army air raid shelter during World War II.

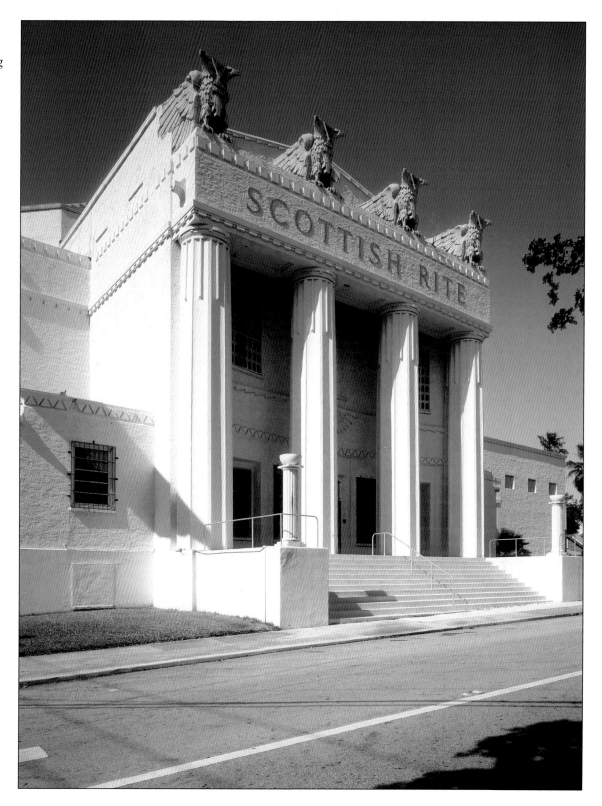

Right: With its striped classical columns and distinctive ziggurat roof, this unique building is still the meeting place for the Masons. Each of the temple's decorative elements has special meaning for them. The massive pillars at the entrance are thirty-two feet high, in reference to their vaulted thirty-two degree honor. Double eagles are used in various places and the symbolic miter and trowel are frequently encountered.

Begun in 1924 and completed in 1925, the old Miami News Tower is one of Miami's most beloved buildings. Governor James M. Cox of Ohio, who bought the paper following his unsuccessful 1920 presidential campaign, hired the New York firm of Schultze and Weaver to design the instant landmark. Patterned after Spain's Giralda tower, it was the first of three Schultze and Weaver South Florida buildings that sported similar pinnacles.

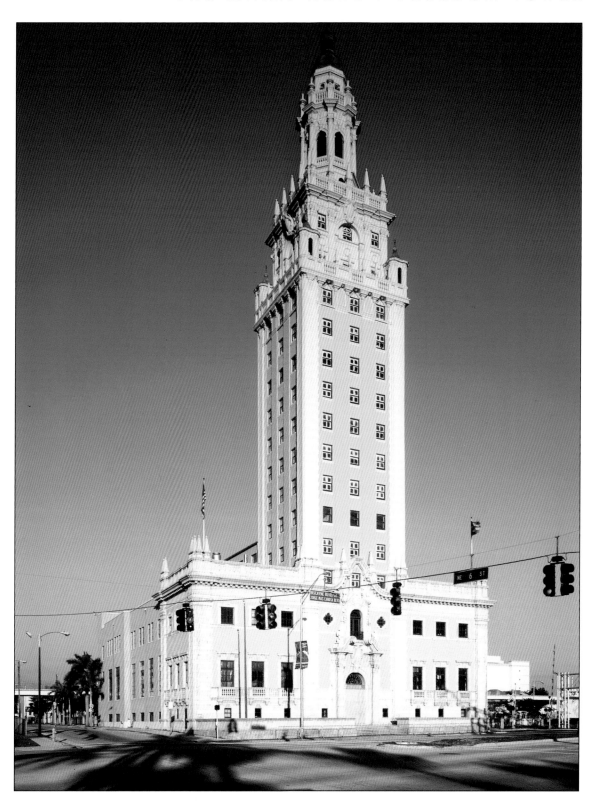

After the *Miami News* moved out in 1957, the building remained vacant until the 1960s, when it took on a new role as a refugee center for hundreds of thousands of Cubans fleeing Communist Cuba. Dubbed the Freedom Tower, it became Miami's Ellis Island. It faced an uncertain future until the influential Cuban American National Foundation acquired it and restored it for use as a Cuban museum and enduring symbol of freedom.

Below: The newly pumped up Biscayne Boulevard was not finished when the devastating 1926 hurricane struck the unsuspecting city. On the morning of September 18, the wide thoroughfare—with ships strewn about like toy boats—looked more like a yacht basin than a street. After the storm, Miami's new skyline, including the Ingraham Building still a skeleton (left), would remain mostly unchanged until the mid-1950s.

Right: Biscayne Boulevard is still one of Miami's most beautiful streets. For a few years after the One Biscayne Tower (center) was completed in 1973, it was the tallest building in Miami and the harbinger of the new skyline. The Metromover that connects the Brickell, Omni, and downtown area opened in 1986. The Arquitectonica-designed American Airlines Arena, seen in the distance, made its debut on the eve of the new millennium.

Left: In 1904, Dade County built its first real courthouse. Constructed from coral rock, the neoclassical, two-story building had an impressive dome and an elegant portico reminiscent of a Greek temple. By 1925, it was clear that the twenty-year-old building could not handle the Boom-induced crowds that descended upon it. Because of the crush to record the multitude of real estate transactions, the new courthouse was built around the old one, where business continued as long as possible.

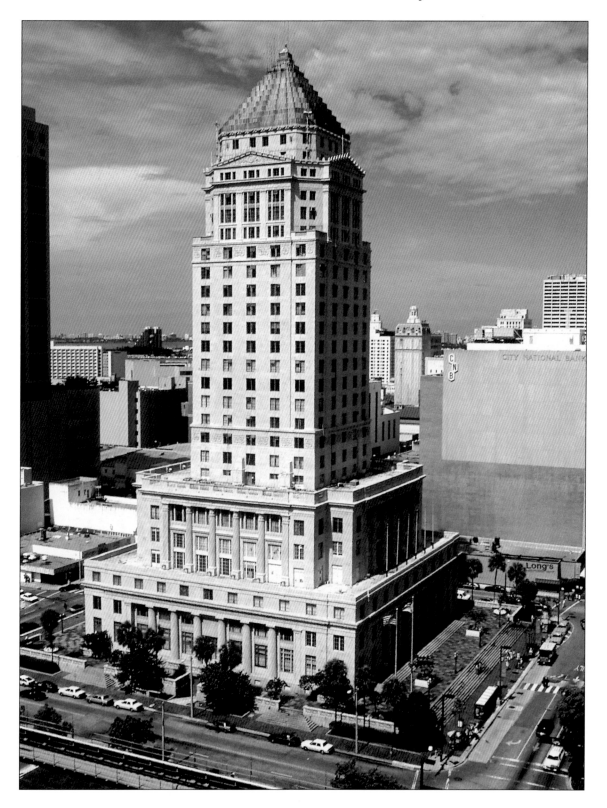

Right: Miamians believed that their impressive skyscraper courthouse, completed in 1928, befitted their recently acquired big-city image. Designed by A. Ten Eyck Brown and August Geiger, the stately neoclassical structure was the Boom's last gasp. For many years, it was Miami's tallest building. Carefully restored in recent years, this National Register building remains a sentinel from the past and a link between the old and the new.

Between 1926 and 1952, the 241-foot *Prins Valdemar* was a Miami landmark on the northern edge of Bayfront Park. It was called "the ship that stopped the Boom" because for a month in early 1926, it capsized and blocked the Miami harbor, causing a shortage of building materials. Towed to a permanent home on Sixth Street, it remained there, serving as a restaurant and aquarium, until it was dismantled and towed away in 1952.

The state-of-the-art American Airlines Arena opened on December 31, 1999, with the Gloria Estefan Millennium Concert Spectacular. Located just north of where the old *Prins Valdemar* once rested, the new Arquitectonica-designed arena brings new life to Biscayne Boulevard. At the rear overlooking Biscayne Bay is Gloria and Emilio Estefan's pineapple-topped Bongos, a tropical-themed Cuban café well known for its fine food and hot dancing.

Riverside was Miami's first subdivision west of the Miami River. One of its most prominent landmarks is the imposing Firestone service station. Built in 1929 under the personal supervision of Harvey S. Firestone, who had a mansion on Miami Beach, it was billed as the largest Firestone facility in the world and was considered his favorite store. It also sported the largest neon sign in Florida.

Although Riverside has been transformed into a vibrant Latin Quarter and many of its historic buildings have been demolished, the Firestone service station still dominates the corner of Flagler Street and Twelfth Avenue. After the building was sold to Walgreens, preservationists convinced the company to retain the old structure, thus guaranteeing its continued presence as an enduring and beloved neighborhood icon.

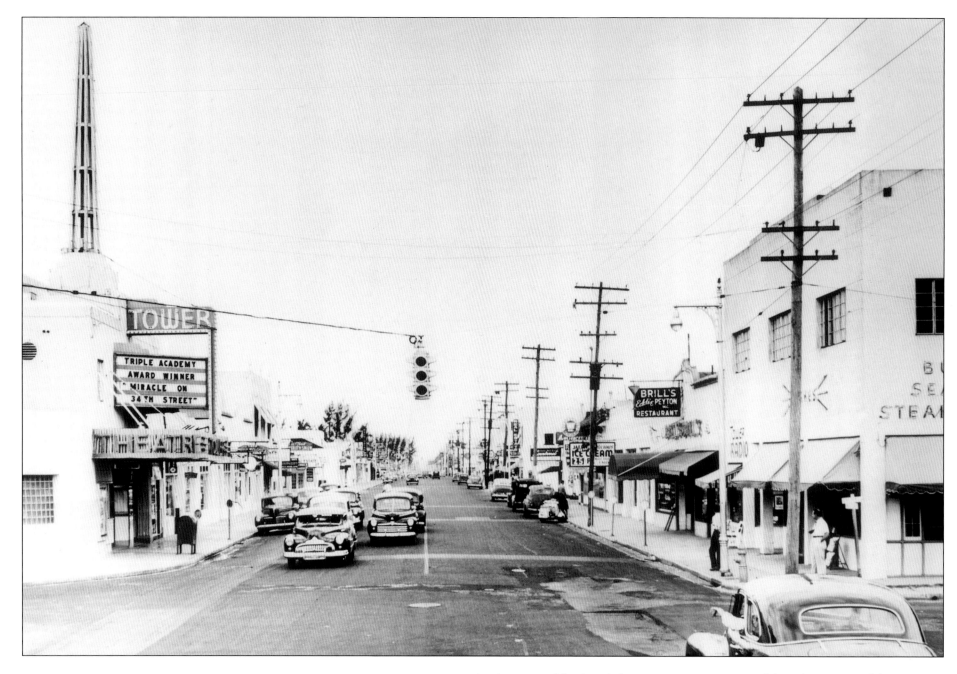

A vibrant neighborhood shopping area grew up on Miami's portion of the Tamiami Trail (SW Eighth Street). Restaurants, shops, and mom-and-pop stores lined the busy street. One of the trail's most popular gathering places was the Tower Theater, built in 1926. In 1931, the Wolfson-Meyer Theater Company (Wometco) hired architect Robert Law Weed to transform it into a little Art Deco gem. The renovation launched Weed's career as a noted theater architect.

After the arrival of the Cuban refugees in the early 1960s, the trail became known as Calle Ocho—the heart of Little Havana. The City of Miami has recently restored the Tower Theater and refurbished Domino Park (left), a popular enclave for elderly Cubans who enjoy playing the traditional game. Each March, Calle Ocho Open House brings more than a million people to the area for a lively Latin street festival.

When this photograph was taken in 1951, the Port of Miami, seen here, was located at the site of today's Bicentennial Park. The main terminal was little more than a warehouse (right). The bay was filled in after the port moved to Dodge Island in 1965. The Miami skyline—from the distinctive Miami News Tower (right) to the cluster of Biscayne Boulevard Hotels (left)—had changed little since the late 1920s.

Today's skyline bears no resemblance to the earlier view. The stern of a cruise ship dominates the tip of a greatly enlarged Port of Miami on Dodge Island—the busiest cruise ship port in the world. The old Miami News Tower, now the Freedom Tower, is barely visible behind the new American Airlines Arena (right), and the soaring County Administration Building dwarfs the Miami-Dade County Courthouse. In Miami, "only the sky is changeless."

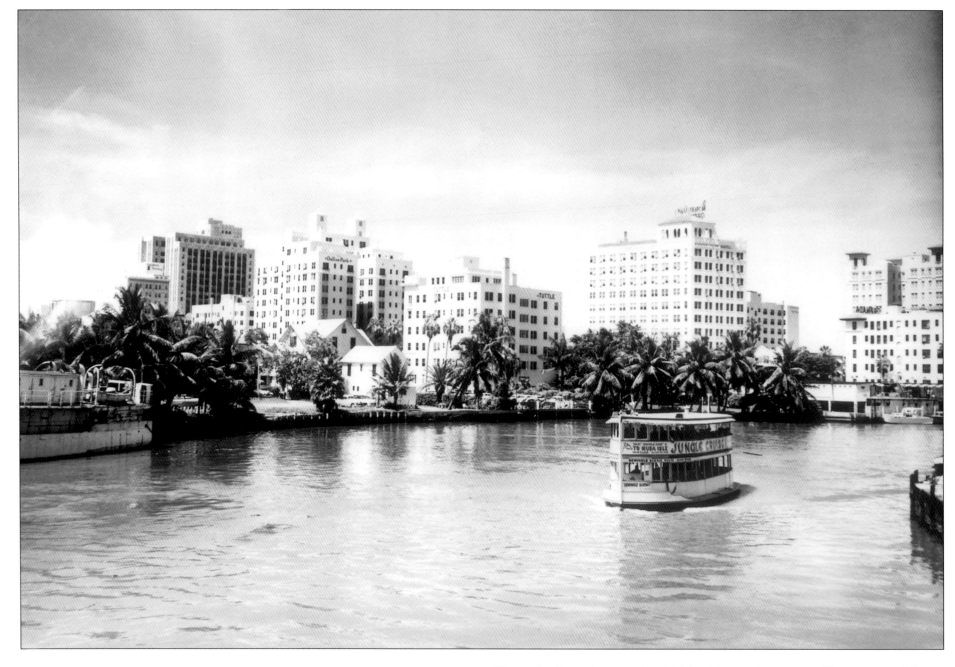

When the Spanish arrived in 1566, a Native American village occupied the north bank of the Miami River (left), which would become Miami 330 years later. From the city's earliest days, visitors took riverboats, like the *Jungle Queen* seen here, to visit Native American tourist attractions upriver. Most of the buildings in this 1940s view, except the Alfred I. DuPont Building (left), have been torn down and replaced with new buildings or parking lots.

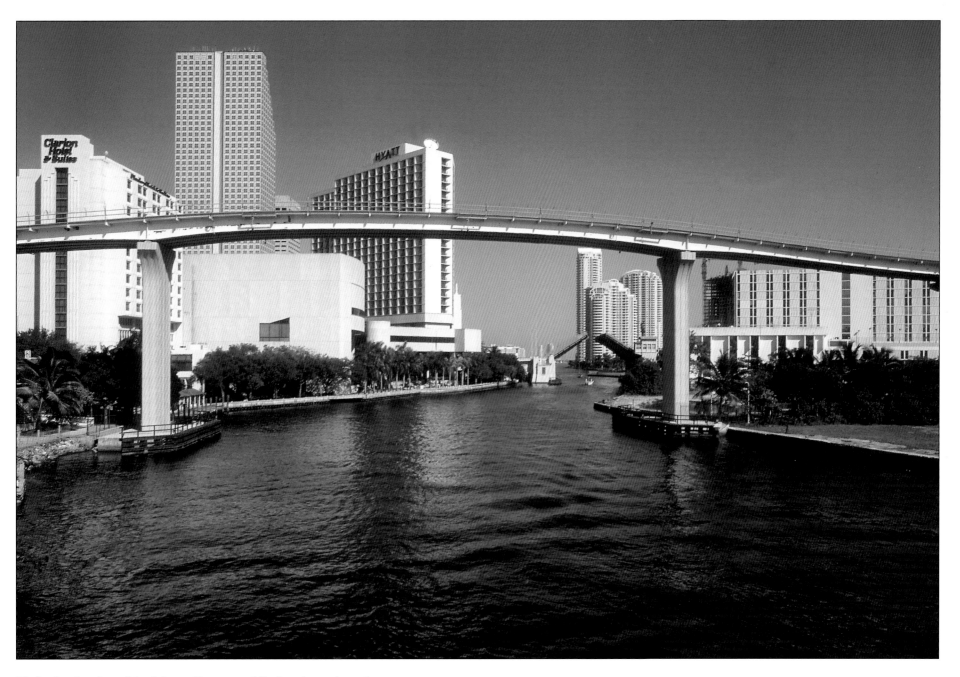

Today both sides of the Miami River are filled with modern skyscrapers. The Metrorail bridge, built in 1984, arcs over the still-active working river. The First Union Tower—the tallest building on the left—sits on land that was once part of Flagler's Royal Palm Park. The riverfront Hyatt Regency Hotel and James L. Knight Conference Center rise on Julia Tuttle's former homesite.

Commodore Ralph M. Munroe, a sailboat designer from Staten Island, was one of Coconut Grove's founders. In 1891, he designed and built this home that he named the "Barnacle." He was so pleased with the design that when his family grew, he simply jacked up the first floor to become the second and built a new first floor underneath. In 1911, three years after the "house raising," he added the semiattached, one-story library.

Thanks to the Munroe family, the Barnacle, which is listed on the National Register of Historic Places, remains one of Miami's most treasured landmarks. In 1973, Munroe's daughter Patty and his son's widow, Mary, spurned developers who offered top dollar for the land and instead sold it for less to the State of Florida. Only at the Barnacle can you reenter the "Era of the Bay"—the time before the railroad arrived and changed everything.

Charles Avenue was the first street in the first black community on the South Florida mainland. Originally called Kebo, its original residents came almost exclusively from the Bahamas. These early families came to work at the Peacock Inn, a tourist hotel that once stood in today's Peacock Park. St. Agnes Missionary Baptist Church, later called Macedonia Baptist (left), founded by Rev. Samuel A. Sampson, was the first Baptist church in the area.

Today Charles Avenue is filled with many historic buildings and sites. Although altered, the original St. Agnes church survives as a reminder of the early days. The descendants of many of the original Charles Avenue families still live in Coconut Grove. In recent years, the community, now called West Grove, has come together to celebrate its roots and preserve its history.

Plymouth Congregational Church traces its history to Isabella Peacock's Sunday school, organized in 1887. Three years later, eighteen Grove pioneers built the Union Chapel on today's McFarlane Road. It became Union Congregational Church in 1897. In 1917, through the efforts of George Merrick (right), chairman of the board of trustees, Rev. George Spalding, and Mr. and Mrs. Arthur Curtiss James, Union Congregational built a new coral rock church, renamed Plymouth Congregation.

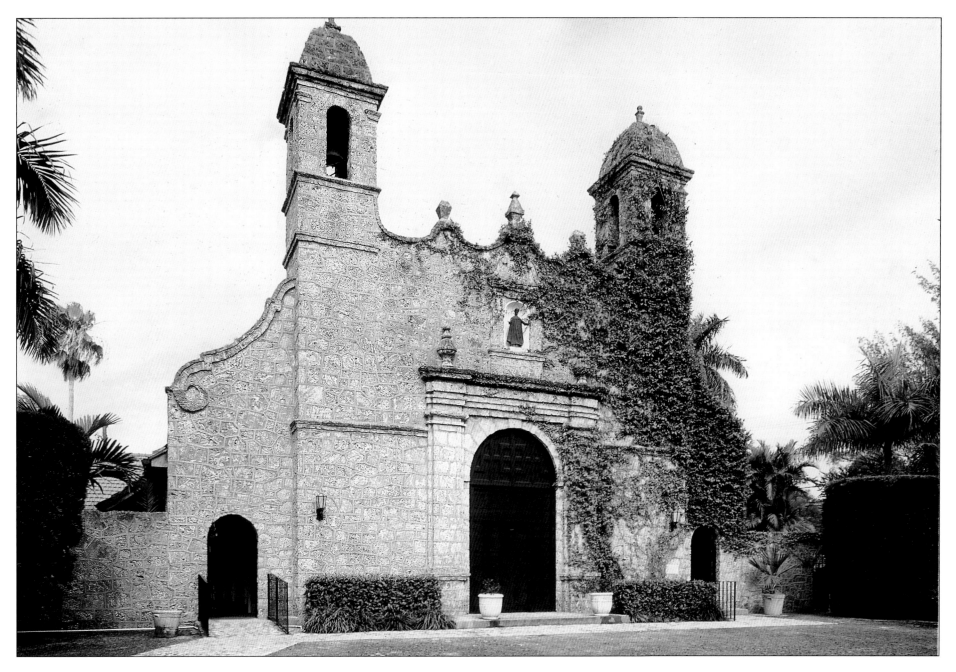

New York architect Clinton McKenzie designed this beautiful church. Spaniard
Felix Rebom, with only a hatchet, a trowel, a T square, and a plumb line, completed
the stonework. The 400-year-old front door came from an old monastery in the
Pyrenees Mountains. Several other historic structures are on its expansive campus
including: Dade County's oldest schoolhouse, several outbuildings from Coconut
Grove's former Matheson Estate, and the original Coconut Grove Waterworks.

In 1891, Flora McFarlane, South Florida's first woman homesteader, organized the Housekeeper's Club for the women of Coconut Grove. The club was the philanthropic and cultural voice of the community and helped define Coconut Grove's special character. In 1905, under the leadership of member Mary Barr Munroe, the club launched the movement to preserve the Everglades. The Walter DeGarmo–designed clubhouse, built in 1921, replaced the original 1897 wooden building.

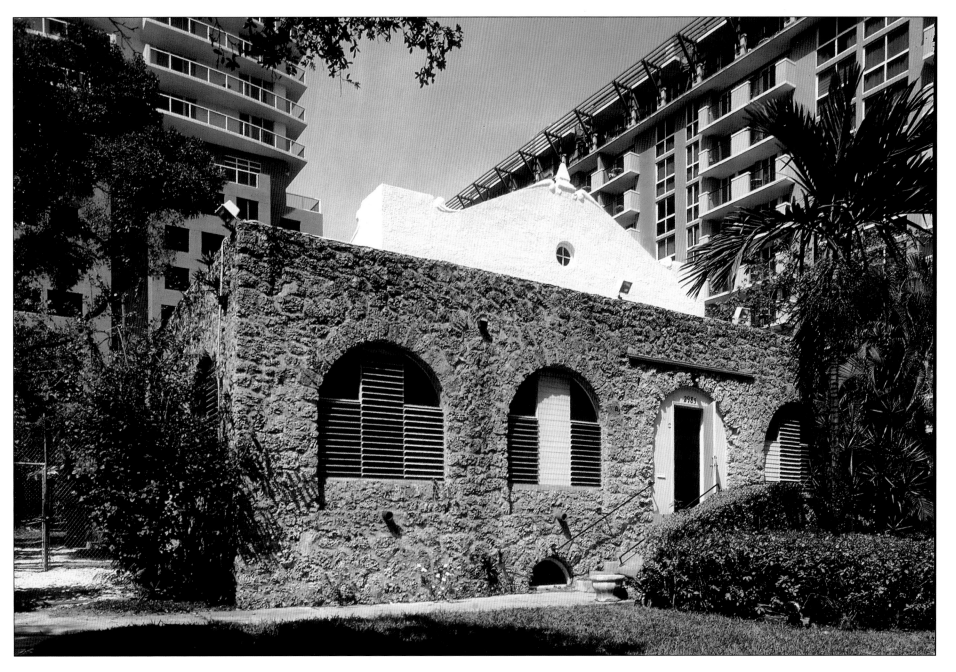

In 1957, the Housekeeper's Club changed its name but not its mission. Shadowed by new high-rise condominiums and threatened by an ever-encroaching highway, the undaunted Woman's Club of Coconut Grove continues to serve the community that spawned it more than 110 years ago. Currently undergoing a restoration, the simple clubhouse, so much a part of Coconut Grove's past, survives as a highly visible community anchor in a sea of turbulent change.

The Coconut Grove Library is the oldest library in Dade County. It was founded in 1895 by the Pine Needles Club, a junior women's club organized by Mary Barr Munroe. It operated out of the upstairs storeroom of Charles Peacock & Sons General Store for six years until Ralph M. Munroe donated the land in 1901, and the men of the community built the new building next to the Union Chapel (left).

The Coconut Grove Library operated independently until 1957 when it became a branch library of what was eventually the Miami-Dade Library system. In 1963, T. Trip Russell designed the current building, incorporating the defining features of the original library into the new structure. Both the American Institute of Architects and the American Library Association honored his design. Although the scene around it has changed, it remains a popular and enduring Coconut Grove institution.

IDACK FLORIDA SCHOOL, COCONUT GROVE, FLA

Perched high on the ridge overlooking Biscayne Bay, the Pagoda derives its name from the pagoda-style building built by Paul C. Ransom in 1902. Ransom, a New York lawyer and educator, opened Pine Knot Camp for boys here in 1896. In 1903, he transformed it into the Adirondack-Florida School, the nation's first two-campus boarding school. Students spent the fall and spring quarters in the Adirondacks and the winter quarter in Coconut Grove.

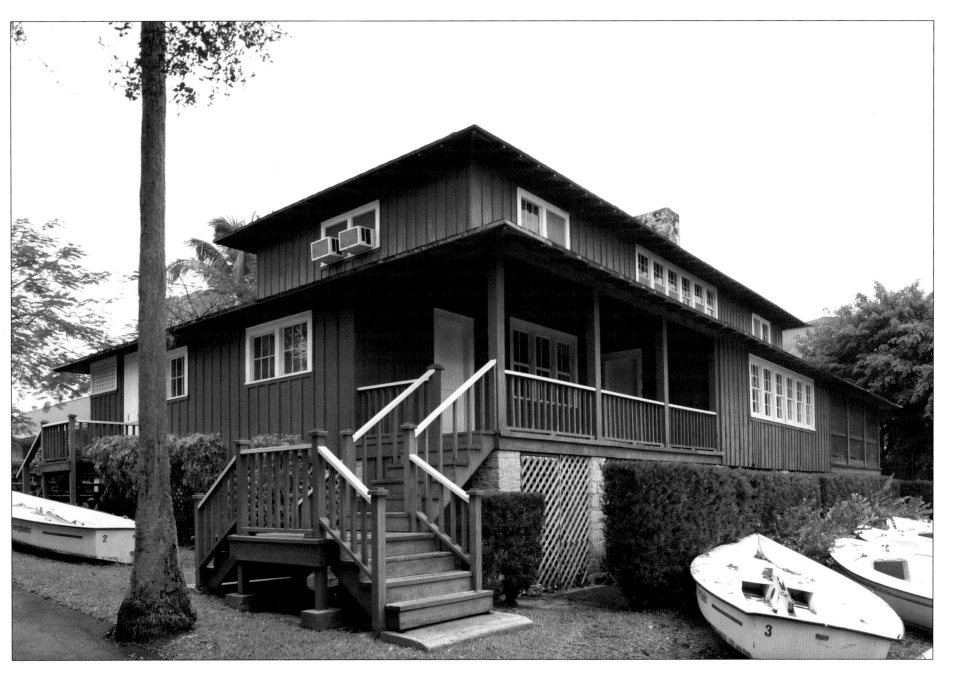

In 1947, the school closed its Adirondack campus but continued operating in Coconut Grove as Ransom School. In 1974, it merged with Everglades School for Girls and became Ransom Everglades. Today the school has two campuses and almost 900 students in grades six through twelve. The beautifully restored Pagoda is considered "the embodiment of the Ransom Everglades tradition" and a living reminder of the school's illustrious past.

In 1912, James Deering, heir to International Harvester, purchased 180 acres of virgin hammock from Mary Brickell. Architect F. Burrell Hoffman Jr. and his associate Paul Chalfin worked closely with Deering to create Vizcaya, a seventy-room Italian villa on the shores of Biscayne Bay. Deering moved into the house in 1916, but five years passed before its expansive gardens, designed by Diego Suarez, were completed.

In 1952, Dade County purchased the estate from the Deering heirs for one million dollars and opened it as a museum. Every year, nearly 200,000 people visit this National Historic Landmark. It has also welcomed such international dignitaries as Queen Elizabeth II of England, King Juan Carlos and Queen Sofia of Spain, Presidents Reagan and Clinton, and Pope John Paul II. In 1994, Vizcaya was the site for the historic Summit of the Americas.

In 1917, John Bindley, president of Pittsburgh Steel, commissioned the firm of Kiehnel and Elliot to design a palatial winter home on a ten-acre tract of bay-front land in Coconut Grove. This beautiful mansion, called "El Jardin," is considered one of the earliest and finest examples of Mediterranean Revival architecture in Miami. Bindley's tropical retreat also had lush gardens, elegant outbuildings, and a breathtaking swimming pool.

In 1961, the Society of the Sacred Heart purchased El Jardin and transformed it into the Carrollton School for Girls. Today more than 600 young women from preschool through high school study amid its incomparable splendor. The Bindley house and its historic outbuildings and features are currently undergoing careful restoration and when completed will be a living study of Mediterranean Revival architecture and a testament to historic preservation and adaptive reuse.

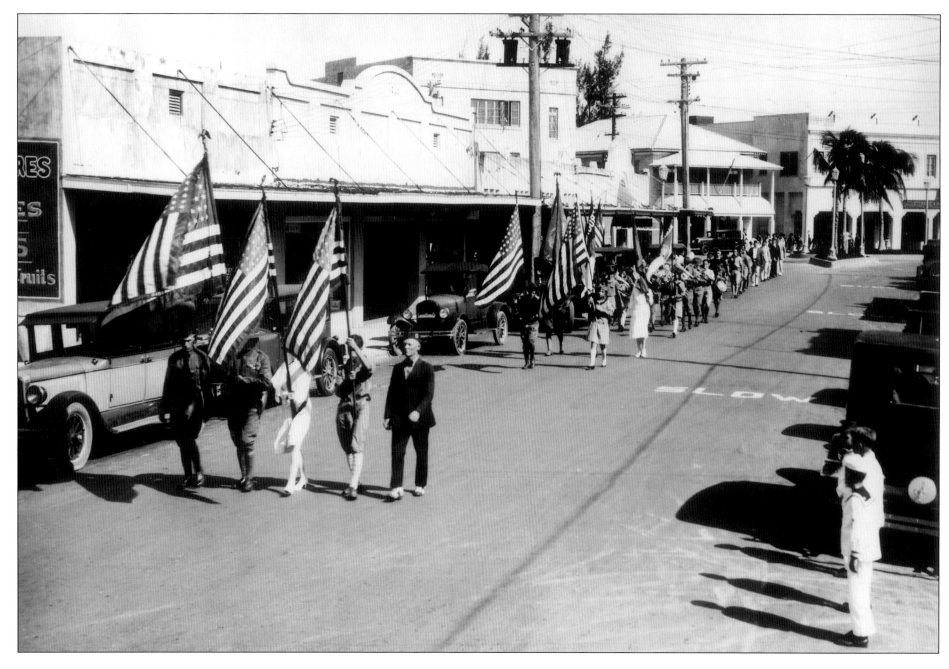

Main Highway and McFarlane Road were the two main business streets in Coconut Grove. In this view, citizens joined in a rousing Armistice Day parade down Main Highway. The building on the left, though altered, still anchors the corner. Sanders Peacock Store, with the second-story balcony, was one of the main general stores in early Coconut Grove. Owner Arthur Sanders was the nephew of Isabella Peacock, the "mother of Coconut Grove."

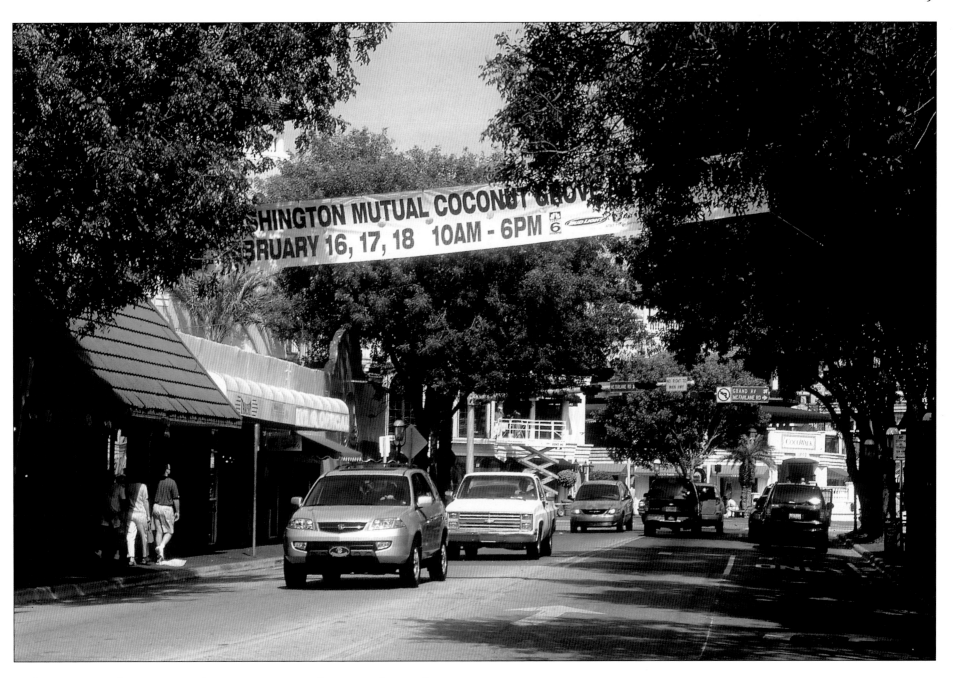

Today's Coconut Grove is an enduring community of artists, sailing enthusiasts, Bohemians, book lovers, and millionaires. Since its founding, it has been known for its lush green environment and "live and let live" philosophy. The Sanders Peacock Store is long gone and CocoWalk, a Mediterranean-themed shopping, restaurant, and entertainment complex, has taken its place. Each February, the Coconut Grove Arts Festival draws thousands of art lovers to the Grove.

When completed in 1931, the Pan American Seaplane Base at Dinner Key, with its daily flights to Latin America and the Caribbean, launched Miami as the "Gateway Between the Americas." Many famous people, including President Franklin D. Roosevelt, flew from here on the "Flying Clippers." Tourists and residents flocked to ogle the ever-present luminaries and enjoy the drama and spectacle of the Clipper's splashdown in Biscayne Bay.

After Pan American Airways abandoned their seaplane operation, the City of Miami purchased the Dinner Key base in 1946 for use as a waterfront park. For several years, the former terminal housed marina offices and a restaurant until the city converted it into the Miami City Hall in 1954. Designed in the Streamline Moderne style by well-known architects Delano and Aldrich, its Art Deco features and waterfront location befit Miami's modern image.

George Merrick, founder of Coral Gables, named the city after his boyhood home, built in 1907. Eight years earlier, his father, Solomon G. Merrick, a Congregational Church minister in Massachusetts, purchased a 160-acre homestead that was five miles west of the three-year-old City of Miami. After he and George turned the homestead into a successful grapefruit-growing plantation, his artist wife, Althea, designed this spacious coral rock home for the family.

During the Depression, Ethel Merrick, George's sister, made their home a boardinghouse she called "Merrick Manor." In 1966, W. L. Philbrick purchased the house and formed the Merrick Manor Foundation in an attempt to preserve it. Threatened with decay and demolition, the manor was acquired by the city in 1976. Beautifully restored, it is filled with family memorabilia and the artistic creations of Althea Merrick, her son, Richard, and her brother Denman Fink.

Because George Merrick believed that "beautiful things inspire high ideals in the minds of children," he commissioned the firm of Kiehnel and Elliot to design a grammar school in keeping with his Mediterranean Revival themed community. Particularly suited to South Florida, its airy classrooms are rimmed by arcaded loggias. The original building was completed in 1923 and the beautiful 600-seat auditorium and a second classroom building were added in 1925.

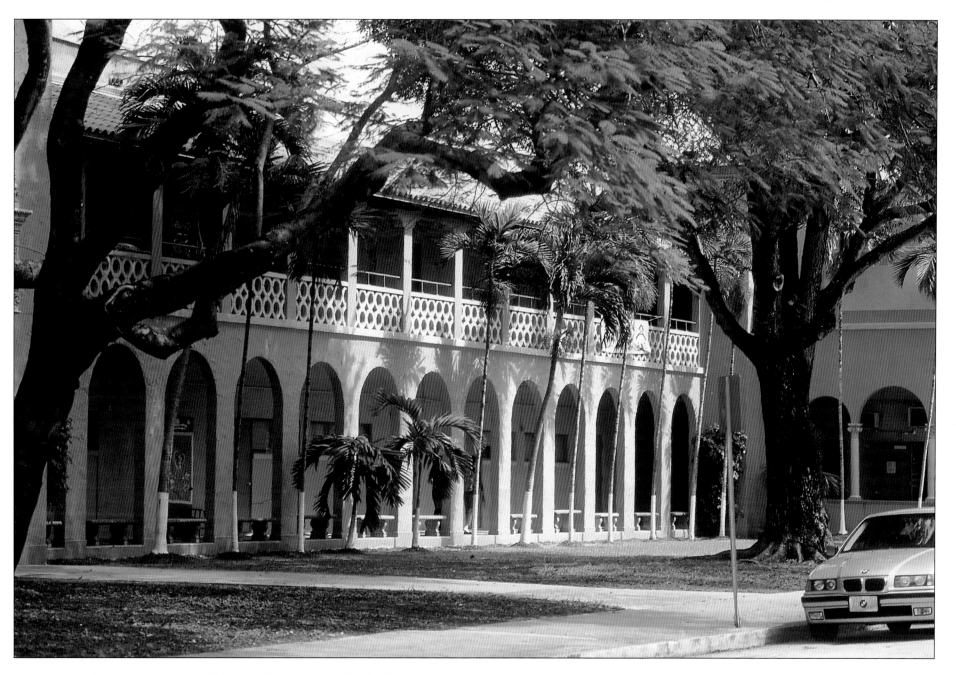

Listed on the National Register of Historic Places, Coral Gables Elementary continues to serve the children of Coral Gables with more than 750 students currently enrolled in preschool through fifth grade. Located in the middle of a growing international city, the student body reflects the area's diversity. In 1993, the central courtyard was dedicated to Eunice P. Merrick, widow of the city's founder, who was on hand to receive the honor.

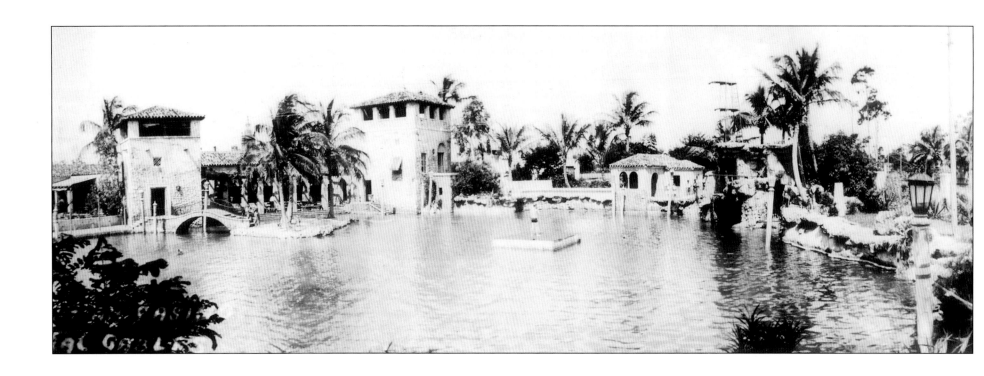

Billed as "the most beautiful swimming hole in the world," Venetian Pool was originally a rock pit from which the Merricks quarried the oolitic limestone, or coral rock, used to build early homes. In 1924, artistic advisor Denman Fink turned the eyesore into a Venetian lagoon with bridges, grottoes, and wide loggias. William Jennings Bryan, three-time presidential candidate, frequently spoke here using his silver-tongued oratory to promote Coral Gables.

Listed on the National Register of Historic Places, Venetian Pool is a living monument to George Merrick and his uncle Denman Fink's original vision for Coral Gables. Generations of local residents and tourists have enjoyed its cool water and inviting architecture. Owned by the city and recently restored, it is arguably the most beautiful and unique municipal swimming pool in the world.

In January 1926, George Merrick and hotelier John McEntee Bowman opened the magnificent Schultze and Weaver–designed Miami Biltmore Hotel, billed as "the last word in the evolution of civilization." Nine months after its much-heralded opening, the 1926 hurricane ushered in an era of hard times. Despite the Depression, the hotel remained open until the Army Air Forces turned it into a hospital during World War II.

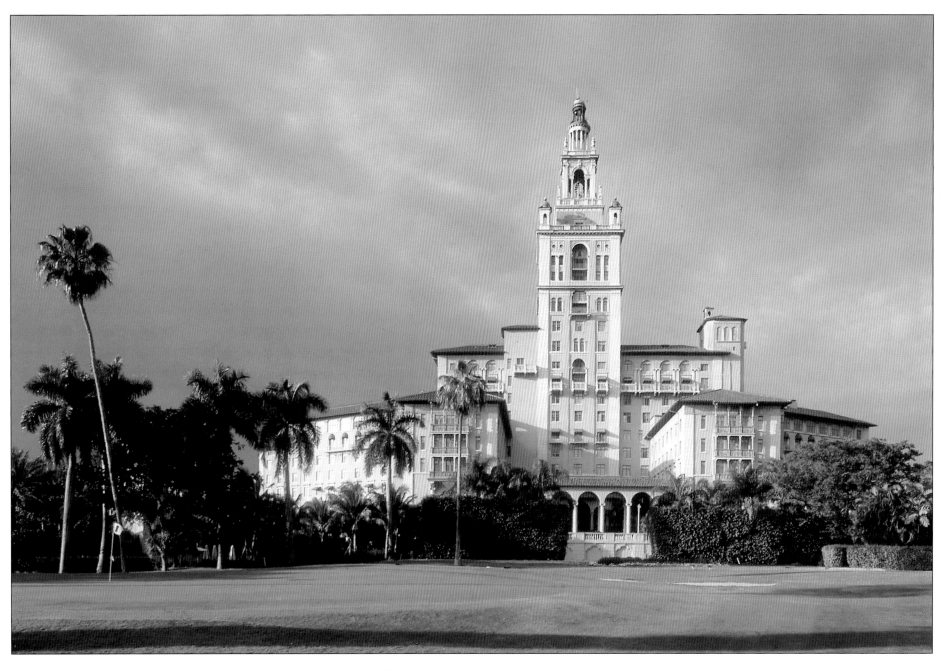

After the war, the Biltmore became the Veterans Hospital. In 1968, the Veterans Hospital closed and the building faced sale and demolition. Acquired by the City of Coral Gables in 1973, the hotel underwent its first restoration in 1985. Today the Seaway Corporation that leases the hotel has recaptured George Merrick's vision. Named a National Historic Landmark, today's Biltmore is an unparalleled resort hotel and conference center.

In 1925, George Merrick launched the University of Miami with his gift of 160 acres of Coral Gables real estate and a pledge of five million dollars. The first building, a beautiful Mediterranean Revival style confection, was named for his father, Solomon G. Merrick. Under construction when the 1926 hurricane struck, it remained an unfinished skeleton for the next twenty years.

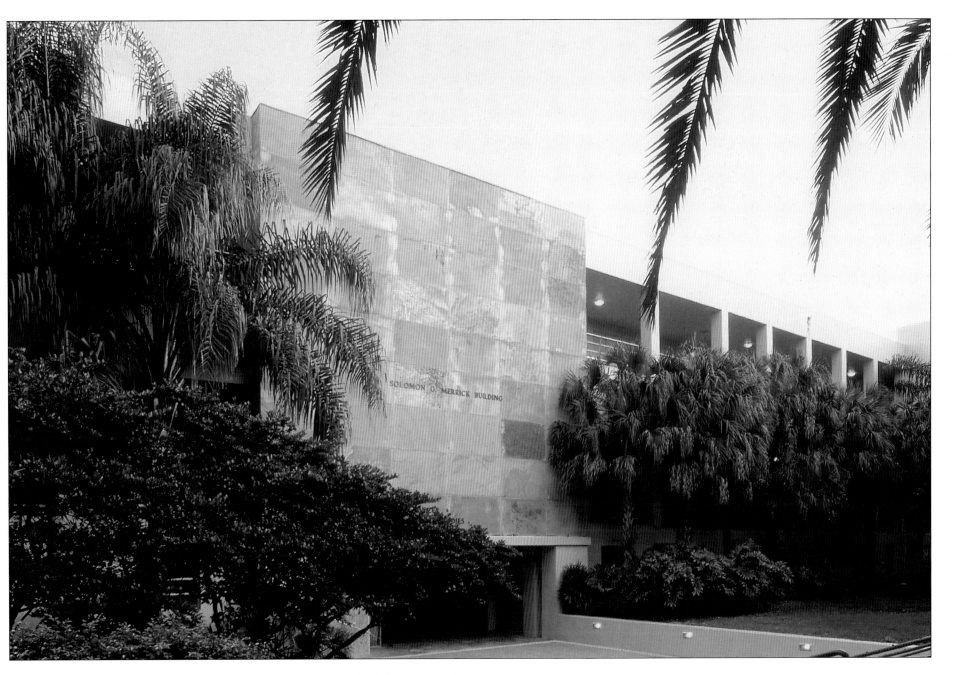

Despite the hurricane, the University of Miami opened as scheduled on October 15, 1926, in a half-finished apartment/hotel that was located several miles from the abandoned campus. "The Skeleton," as it was fondly called, stood alone and covered in vines until 1946, when the University of Miami moved back to its original campus. In 1946, the university completed the Merrick Building, seen here, in a modern style that was noted in national architectural magazines.

George Merrick built the Colonnade, designed by Phineas Paist and Walter DeGarmo, in 1926 as headquarters for his sales operation. Before it was completed, the Boom ended and with it, Merrick's plans. After his Coral Gables Corporation folded, the building had many uses. During World War II, it was a pilot training facility and parachute factory. It also housed a motion picture studio, a gymnasium, and a bank.

In 1985, Intercap Investments saved and completely restored the Colonnade and connected it to a new Spillis Candela–designed hotel and office building. The original Colonnade's impressively restored rotunda became a community gathering place. The modern four-star Omni Colonnade Hotel recalls the historic ambience of the original building through its furnishings, art, and grill, named after "Doc" Dammers, the legendary salesman and first mayor of Coral Gables.

Coral Gables is known for its beautiful gateways and plazas. One of the most impressive is Puerta del Sol (Gate of the Sun). Designed by architects Walter DeGarmo, Phineas Paist, and artist Denman Fink, Douglas Entrance, as it is commonly known today, was part of a planned enclosed Spanish village on a ten-acre site. Although the village was not completed, city officials dedicated the entrance in May 1927.

In 1968, an application to demolish the Douglas Entrance sparked Coral
Gables' first preservation effort. Citizens and architects rallied to save it from
becoming a supermarket parking lot. Spillis Candela, one of Miami's oldest
architectural firms, completed the master plan for the complex, restored the
historic buildings, and designed two new towers around this beautiful central
plaza. It is listed on the National Register of Historic Places.

Ponce de Leon Boulevard was one of the main thoroughfares in George Merrick's master plan for Coral Gables. It was filled with strictly mandated Mediterranean Revival buildings that even included service stations (right). The imposing Coral Gables Theater (right) has been demolished and replaced with a modern high-rise. Merrick also built several small hotels, including the Sevilla (left). This street remained mostly unchanged from the late 1920s until the late 1960s.

In the 1960s, after Coral Gables changed its zoning to allow high-rise buildings, the area underwent a dramatic change—a trend that continues today. The Texaco Building (left) was the first high-rise in the commercial district. Except for a few small structures, the tower of the Sevilla Hotel, now the Hotel Place St. Michel (left), is the last defining historic landmark on a street that once had the ambience of a Spanish town.

Except for the beautiful 1928 City Hall, George Merrick had barely begun to develop Coral Way when the Boom ended. After World War II, Merrick, along with Rebyl Zain, promoted the idea of transforming the mostly barren street into a high-class, modern "Miracle Mile." The idea took hold and the city abandoned Merrick's Mediterranean Revival style requirements. They encouraged more modern designs, including the 1948 Art Deco style Miracle Theatre (left).

Today, Miracle Mile looks much like it did fifty years ago except for newly planted landscaping in the median that blocks the view of City Hall (*see inset*). In 1995, when the Miracle Theatre was threatened with demolition, the city acquired it and designated the Actor's Playhouse as its resident theater company. Soon the face of Miracle Mile will change when Starwood Urban's new $57 million mixed-use project is completed at the eastern end.

During the Boom, James Bright and Glen Curtiss developed Hialeah. Known for its sporting and gaming facilities, the Hialeah Jockey Club thrived for years before Florida legalized pari-mutuel betting in 1931. After Joseph Widener's two million dollar refurbishing, Hialeah Race Course reopened in 1932, billing itself the "Saratoga of the South." Citation won the Flamingo Stakes here in 1948. It is now on the National Register of Historic Places.

Squeezed out by nearby competing tracks, the legendary and still beautiful
Hialeah Race Course saw its last race on May 22, 2001. Facing an uncertain
future, the elegant pavilion, ballroom, three restaurants, and park grounds are
now rented for festivals and social events. The famous flock of flamingos still
lives in the track's infield.

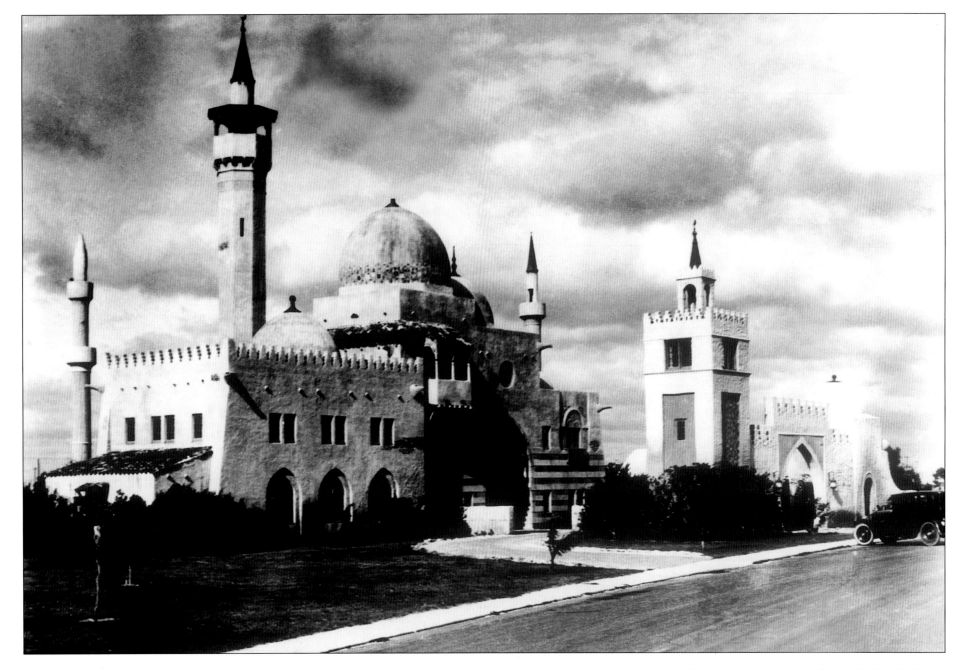

In early 1926, aviation luminary Glen Curtiss announced Opa-locka, the last grandiose project of the Boom. Based on a theme from the *Arabian Nights* and designed by architect Bernhardt Muller, his fantasy subdivision had domed palaces fit for the grandest potentate, surrounded by small homes, each with a distinctive Arabian motif. Nowhere else in America could a person live in a home on Sesame Street with two bedrooms, one bath, and a minaret.

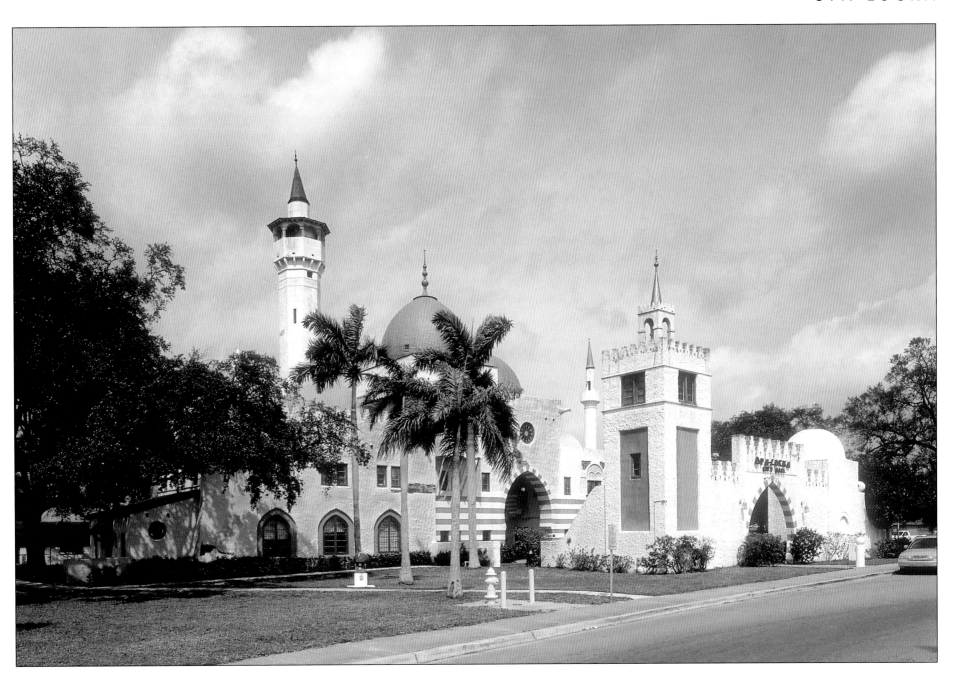

Although Curtiss's vision for a complete Arabian-themed community died with the Boom, many buildings had been completed before the crash. Streets were laid out in the shape of the Islamic crescent moon and named for characters in the *Arabian Nights*. Restored in 1988, Curtiss and Muller's masterpiece, the incomparable Opa-locka City Hall, formerly Curtiss's administration building, survives. Each May, the city hosts the Arabian Nights Festival to celebrate its unique character.

Across Biscayne Bay from Miami, banker brothers J. E. and J. N. Lummus sold land at the south end of the beach as early as 1912. Their property along Ocean Drive became a public park. In the foreground of this 1933 view is Cook's Casino, one of four well-known bathhouses along the shore. The 1927 City Hall (left) and the luxurious Roney Plaza Hotel (center) were built in the Mediterranean Revival style.

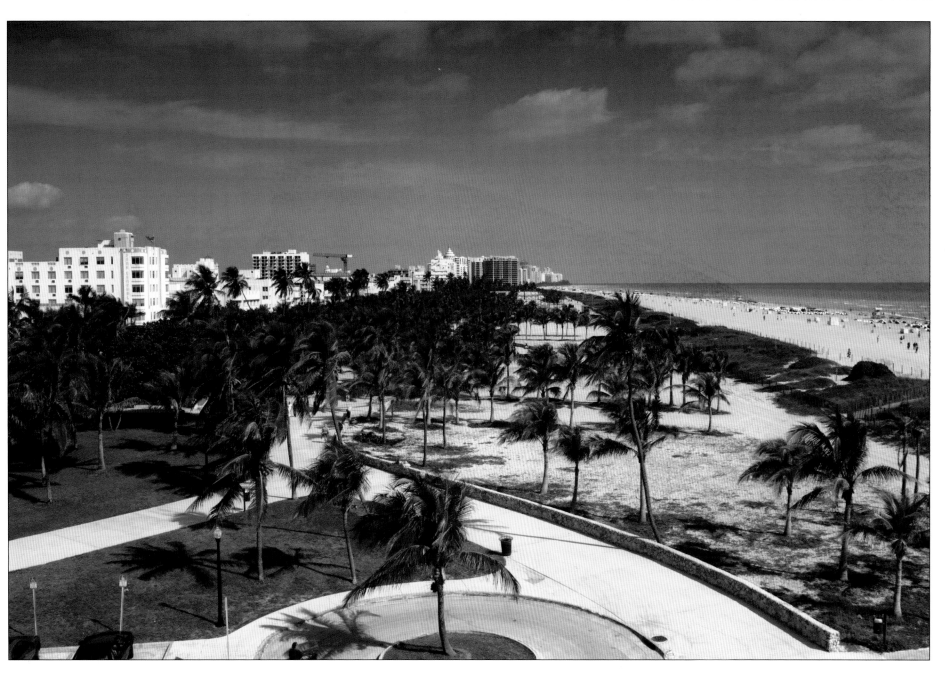

Sand replenishment has widened the beach considerably, but Lummus Park remains the "front yard" of the Miami Beach Architectural District, placed on the National Register of Historic Places in 1979. Also called the "Art Deco District," it contains hundreds of examples of 1930s architecture. Henry Hohauser, the city's most prolific Art Deco architect, designed the Park Central Hotel (left) in 1937. The turret (center) tops the new Loews Miami Beach Hotel.

Avery Smith, who came to Miami from Connecticut, built this house in 1918. When he first explored the deserted oceanfront jungle he said he felt like Robinson Crusoe. Seeing the area's potential, he created the Biscayne Navigation Company, which operated excursion cruises and provided daily ferry service between Miami and the beach. He later purchased and operated Smith's Casino, the beach's first bathhouse that had been built by the unrelated Dick Smith.

The house is built of local oolitic limestone, or coral rock, a popular and inexpensive early building material. Few such structures have survived. In recent years, this little house has been the venue for various restaurants and a beauty spa. Because it is such a rare example of early vernacular architecture and because of its link to Avery Smith, it is a regular stop on walking tours.

In order to transport his avocado crops to market, John S. Collins, an elderly Quaker from New Jersey, created the Collins Canal in 1912, linking Indian Creek to Biscayne Bay. In 1924, the canal inspired this Venetian-style residence complete with gondolas. The house originally served as a model to promote a planned bayfront cooperative apartment called Villa Biscayne, designed by Schultze and Weaver.

Villa Biscayne was never built, but the famous portrait artist Henry Salem Hubbell made the model his home for several years. Today jet-skiers swoop past the house, unaware of its illustrious past. Now split into rental apartments, it is a highlight of the Palm View Historic District, designated by the City of Miami Beach in 1999 as an enclave of exemplary 1920s–1950s residential architecture.

In addition to his canal, John S. Collins built a wooden bridge across Biscayne Bay—the beach's first connection to Miami—in 1913. The elegant "Venetian Way," which was interspersed with islands dredged from bay bottom, replaced the old bridge in 1926. This view looking toward Miami during the causeway's construction shows Trinity Episcopal Church (center) and August Geiger's 1926 Spanish Renaissance style building for the Miami Woman's Club and Flagler Memorial Library (far right).

The Venetian Causeway and its islands are still a popular route and residential neighborhood. On the Miami side, the Miami Woman's Club Building, its future uncertain, is dwarfed by towering hotels and condominiums. The church, now Trinity Cathedral, is still intact but not visible here. The Miami Herald Building (far left) was designed by Naess & Murphy in 1959, modeled after their Chicago Sun-Times Building.

In January 1924, John S. Collins's grandson J. Arthur Pancoast opened the elegant Mediterranean Revival style Pancoast Hotel, Miami Beach's first grand oceanfront hotel. Its architect, Martin L. Hampton, designed many notable buildings in Palm Beach, Miami, and Coral Gables, as well as Miami Beach. During World War II, the Pancoast served as a military hospital. It was demolished in 1953.

Designed by Melvin Grossman and completed in March 1956, the Seville Hotel is an outstanding remnant of Miami Beach's exuberant postwar boom. New, glamorous resort hotels abandoned the pedestrian scale and symmetry of the Art Deco style and outdid one another with rakish angles, bright lights, and fantasy themes. The Seville is now a highlight of the Collins Waterfront Historic District, designated in 2001.

Carl Fisher, a self-made millionaire from Indianapolis, was Miami Beach's greatest early developer. He built five hotels, and the Nautilus, on Biscayne Bay at Forty-third Street, was one of the grandest. Designed by New York architects Schultze and Weaver and completed in 1925, it had its own polo fields (right), radio station, and rental cottages on Collins Island (foreground). Fisher built no hotels on the oceanfront, and sold his lots there to his millionaire friends for their private estates.

The Nautilus became a military hospital during World War II and never returned to use as a hotel. In 1946, the local Jewish community established Mount Sinai Hospital, which moved into the vacated Nautilus Hotel in 1948. The Julia Tuttle Causeway (foreground) gave Miami Beach another bridge to Miami in 1959. As Mount Sinai Medical Center expanded, the outdated Nautilus building was demolished in 1968.

Oilman James Snowden was one of Carl Fisher's real estate partners. In the early 1920s, he built this mansion (foreground) on the beach at Forty-fourth Street, then just within the northern city limits. It was the southernmost estate on "Millionaires' Row" that extended north to the Bath Club at Sixtieth Street. Tire magnate Harvey Firestone purchased the home in 1924 and it became better known as the Firestone Estate.

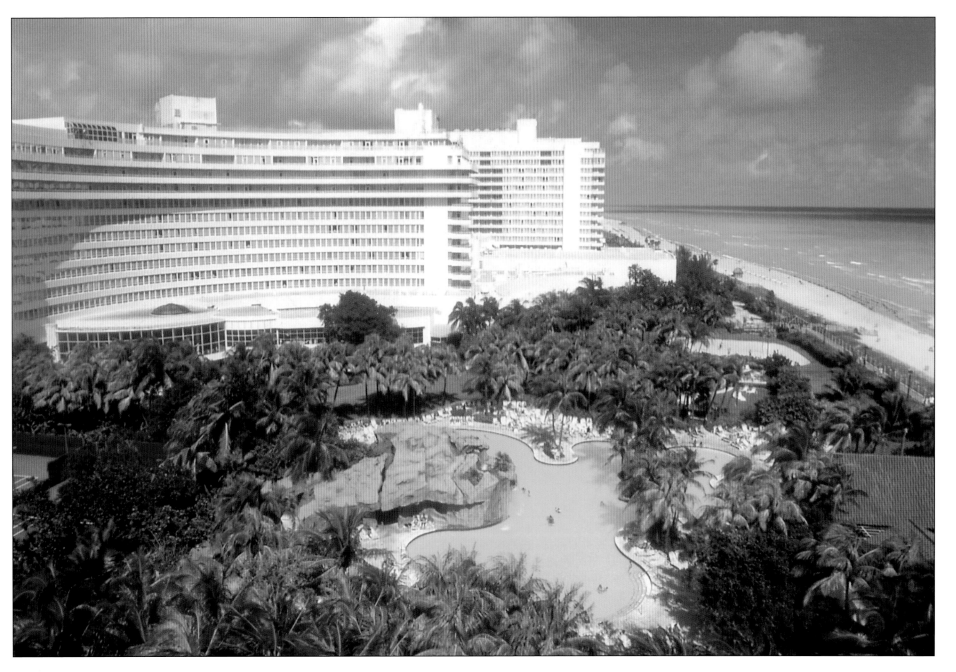

After World War II, all the mansions on Millionaires' Row were demolished in favor of luxury high-rise apartments and resort hotels. In 1954 the Firestone Estate was the first to fall, but a new landmark replaced it—the Morris Lapidus–designed Fontainebleau Hotel. Reviled by architecture critics at the time, it was an immediate hit with tourists and became an icon of Miami Beach glamour and glitz. It has been a Hilton Resort since 1978.

The 1905 opening of Government Cut severed the southern tip of the beach and created an island that developer Carl Fisher later acquired. In 1925, William K. Vanderbilt II, president of his great-grandfather's New York Central Railroad, built a winter estate here with a mansion designed by Palm Beach architect Maurice Fatio. Vanderbilt traveled the world on his yacht, the *Alva*, seen here, to study marine life. The County (now MacArthur) and Venetian Causeways are in the distance.

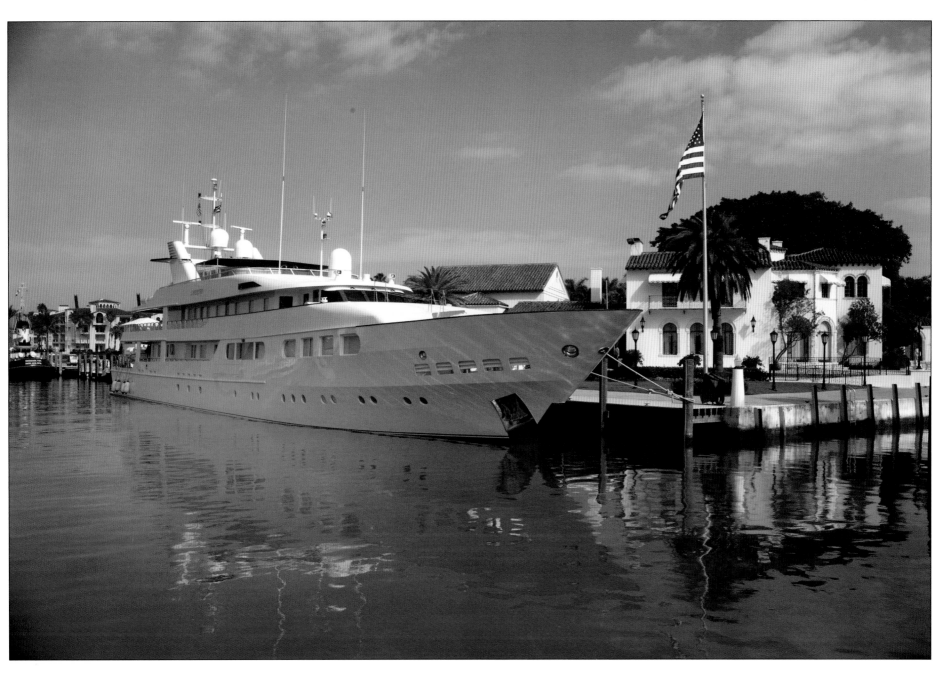

Since the mid-1980s, Fisher Island has been developed as a private club, inn, and luxury condominium village accessible only by boat, seaplane, or helicopter. The original mansion now serves as a clubhouse, restaurant, and ballroom. The 216-acre island has six restaurants, its own post office, firehouse, bank, market, a nine-hole golf course, and a luxury spa. Residents use golf carts for quiet transport.

To attract young, active tourists to Miami Beach in the 1920s, Carl Fisher invested heavily in sports—especially polo, golf, and speedboat racing. His first golf course originally extended from Lincoln Road northward to Twenty-eighth Street. August Geiger, Fisher's favorite architect, designed this clubhouse in 1916. It is nearly identical to the Miami City Hospital ("the Alamo") that he designed a year earlier.

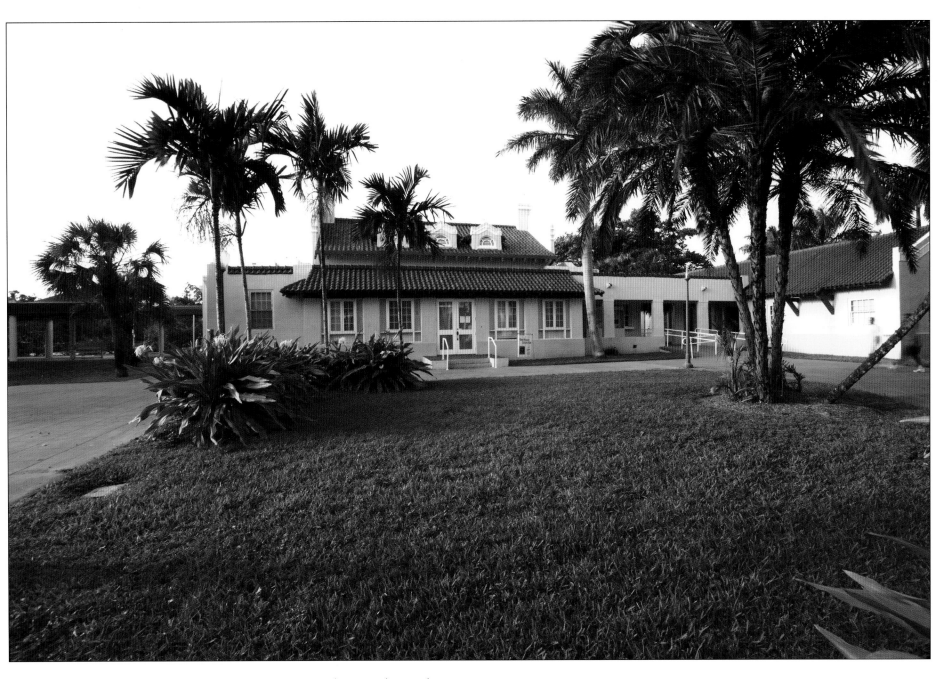

Today, the Miami Beach Convention Center occupies what was the southern half of the golf course, but the original clubhouse still stands on the south bank of the Collins Canal at Twenty-first Street. It is a locally designated historic site and one of the oldest buildings in the city. In recent years it has served as an art school for the Bass Museum and a community theater.

Carl Fisher built Miami Beach's first public school in 1920. Before it opened, Miami Beach children either attended private schools or took the long trip across the bay to public schools in Miami. H. George Fink, George Merrick's cousin and later a prominent Coral Gables architect, designed this Mediterranean Revival style school with open arcades to take advantage of the ocean breezes.

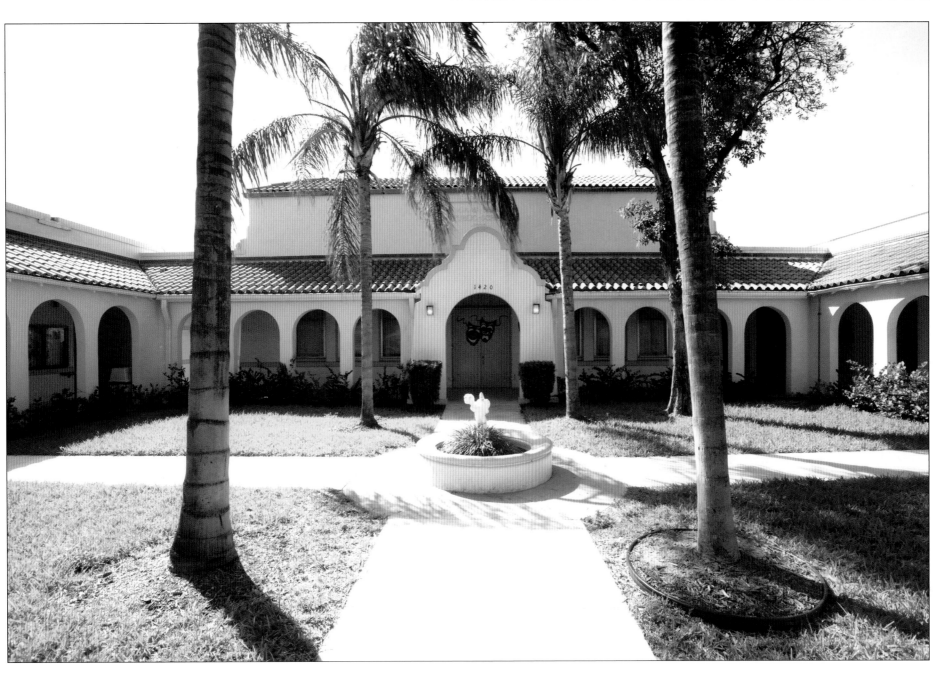

August Geiger designed many later additions to the original school, including
a high school named for Carl Fisher's mother, Ida. Now also named for Leroy
D. Fienberg, a principal in the 1960s, Fienberg-Fisher Elementary School has
students from fifty countries in preschool through sixth grade. The arcades are
still pleasant, and air conditioners were added in the 1960s. The original
decorative friezes along the parapet have not survived.

Newton B. T. Roney created this two-block stretch of exotic fantasy in 1924. Roney, a lawyer from Camden, New Jersey, moved to Miami in 1918 and became prominent in banking and real estate. Espanola Way, also known as Roney's Spanish Village, was planned as an artists' colony. Architect Robert A. Taylor designed its shops, apartments, and hotels in pure Mediterranean Revival style. The following year, Roney would open his landmark Roney Plaza Hotel at Twenty-third Street.

In later years, Al Capone's gambling syndicate operated from Espanola Way, and Desi Arnaz is said to have started the rumba craze here. The 1980s television series *Miami Vice* used this atmospheric street as a ready-made set. Today, it remains a favorite Miami Beach locale and still has a Bohemian flavor with art galleries, shops, outdoor cafés, and street festivals. A youth hostel occupies one of the original hotels.

Mangrove forests covered most of the beach when Carl Fisher began creating his winter playground for other wealthy northerners. His Lincoln Road was cleared around 1912 (*see inset*) and soon became the town's social center. The tall building in the 1927 view was designed by August Geiger in 1924 for Fisher's own realty office. The Dowling Building (far left) housed Bonwit Teller and later, Saks Fifth Avenue. Across the street, the Bastian Building contained small shops and offices.

In 1960, architect Morris Lapidus redesigned Lincoln Road as one of the nation's
first pedestrian malls. After a severe economic slump, restoration efforts in the
1980s began to revive it. Fisher's office building, now the Van Dyke, houses a
popular restaurant and jazz bar; the Dowling Building has been beautifully
restored; and the Bastian Building is currently undergoing restoration. Today
Lincoln Road vies with Ocean Drive as Miami Beach's most popular scene.

As early as the 1920s, Lincoln Road, with its fashionable shops, was called "the Fifth Avenue of the South." Besides the latest merchandise, the stores also showed off their architecture—using it as a form of advertising. This building was the 1929 showroom or "salon" for Cadillac, Fleetwood, and La Salle automobiles. Over the door, a carved bas-relief of cars, airplanes, lightning bolts, and the Cadillac crest exuberantly celebrated the machine age.

For decades, plaster cladding had hidden this forgotten frieze—the earliest example of Art Deco yet identified on Miami Beach. Renovations in June 2000 brought it back to light. This is one of several Lincoln Road buildings that now incorporate restored elements from the 1920s into twenty-first century additions.

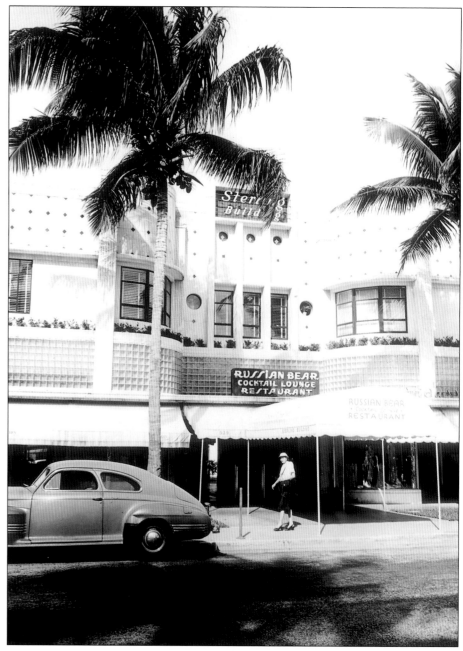

Above: In 1928, architect Alexander Lewis designed a pair of Mediterranean Revival style commercial buildings on the 900 block of Lincoln Road that faced each other across a courtyard. This Packard showroom occupied part of the eastern building and was one of several elegant automobile salons on Lincoln Road. Both Lewis and another architect, Victor Nellenbogen, had their offices in this complex.

Above: In 1941, Victor Nellenbogen fused the two original buildings into a single Art Deco style structure called the Sterling Bulding. The original courtyard became an arcade enclosed in front by a second-story wall. The Russian Bear restaurant was an early tenant.

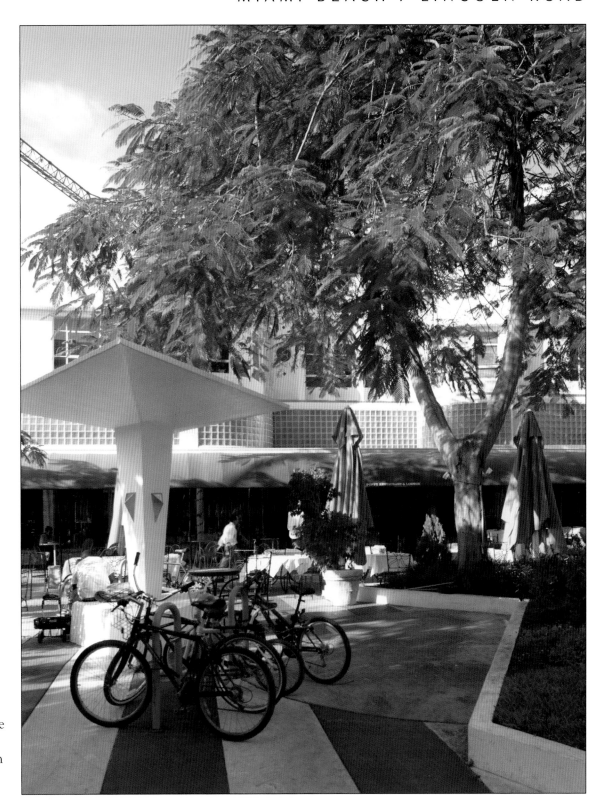

Mitchell Wolfson Jr., founder of the Wolfsonian/FIU, restored the Sterling Building in 1986, launching the revival of Lincoln Road. The Russian Bear is still the name of a café in the building, which also houses a bookstore and other shops and offices. Its blue-and-white facade with a neon-lit swath of glass block is a local landmark.

Early in 1942, as the nation mobilized for World War II, Miami Beach became a major training center for the U.S. Army Air Forces. Tourists left and eighty-five percent of the city's hotels became barracks. By 1945, the city had hosted half a million troops—both new recruits in ninety-day training and combat veterans who came here for processing and reassignment. The streets, including Lincoln Road, seen here, rang with marching feet and singing soldiers.

Today bicyclers and roller bladers whisk along the old marching route. John S. Collins's grandson, architect Russell T. Pancoast, designed the Mead Building for Bonwit Teller in 1928. Its pointed arch has been reconstructed as an entrance to a Victoria's Secret store. The 1924 Bastian Building (background) is currently undergoing restoration.

Joseph Eisener, Carl Fisher's former salesman, built the Deauville Hotel in 1925. It was a gaudy hotel and entertainment complex that boasted Florida's largest swimming pool. But its remote location on the empty beach at Sixty-seventh Street hindered its success. Bernarr Macfadden, a health and diet guru known for outlandish publicity stunts, leased it in 1936 and ran it as the Macfadden Deauville health spa.

The old Deauville was demolished in 1956 and in its place, Melvin Grossman designed the new Deauville Hotel. With its soaring carport, marble lobby, glass-walled dining room, shopping arcade, and even an ice-skating rink, it was the epitome of the glamorous postwar Miami Beach resort-style hotels. A long list of celebrities performed here, including the Beatles in 1964. The hotel, now the Radisson Deauville Resort, retains most of its 1950s architecture.

Henri Levy was a French Jewish immigrant who started a movie theater chain in Cincinnati. He moved his family to Miami Beach in 1922 and soon joined in the real estate boom. One of his developments, named for his homeland, was Normandy Isle in Biscayne Bay at Seventy-first Street. This fountain in a central plaza was one of the first structures built there, lending an air of French elegance to a largely deserted island.

The streets of Normandy Isle still have French names, but most of today's residents are Hispanic. From its inception, a number of factors have hampered the development of this section of Miami Beach, but the area is now undergoing a renaissance. The Normandy Isle Fountain has been adopted as a neighborhood icon and the surrounding plaza is the setting for a farmers market and various cultural events.

For Miami, the heady days of the Boom came to an end on September 17–18, 1926, when a monster hurricane with peak winds of 132 miles per hour pummeled the area. More than one hundred died and thousands were injured. Sand was two feet deep all along Ocean Drive and hundreds of buildings, like the Roosevelt Apartments (left and center) and its neighbor, the Coronado (right), suffered heavy damage.

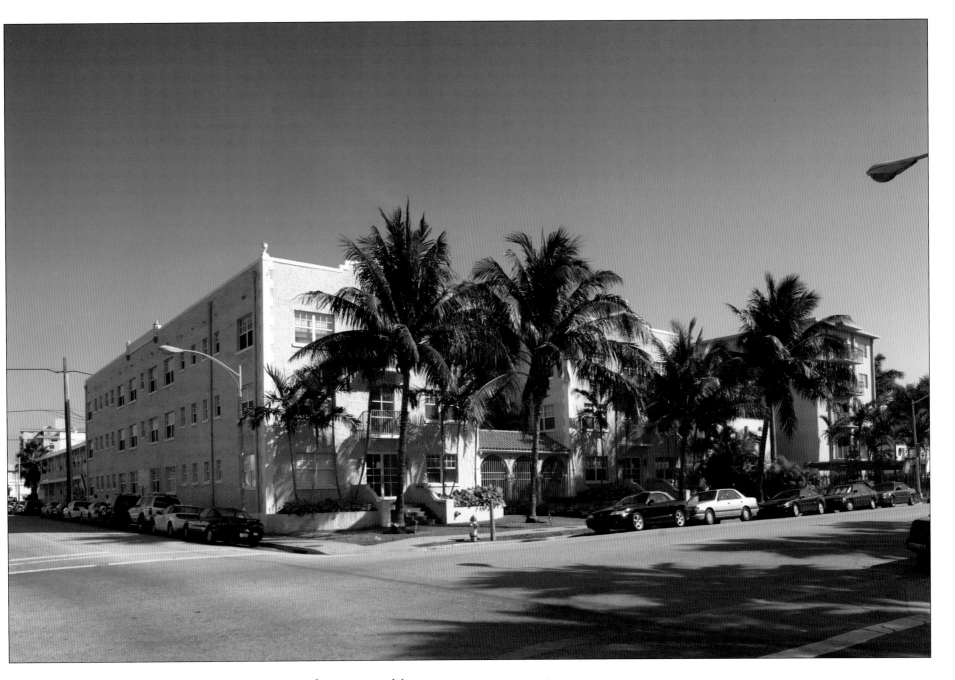

Buildings that survived the 1926 hurricane are special treasures in Miami Beach today. The Roosevelt, designed by Martin Hauri in 1925, also weathered Hurricane Andrew in 1992. Since then, Miami-Dade County has enacted stringent new building codes. The Roosevelt was extensively renovated in 1993 and is now a condominium with no trace of its past troubles.

In 1927, Martin L. Hampton designed this grand Mediterranean Revival style building on Washington Avenue to serve as Miami Beach's second city hall. The city had outgrown the first—a small frame building on Fifth Street—and Carl Fisher intended this impressive structure to restore confidence in Miami Beach after the previous year's devastating hurricane. The north wing originally served as the city's main fire station.

This building no longer serves as city hall but houses court facilities and other offices. The present Miami Beach City Hall was built in 1975 on Seventeenth Street. Old City Hall was beautifully restored in 1987 by Borelli, Frankel, Blitstein Joint Ventures, who at the same time designed the new police headquarters (left), using updated Art Deco design elements.

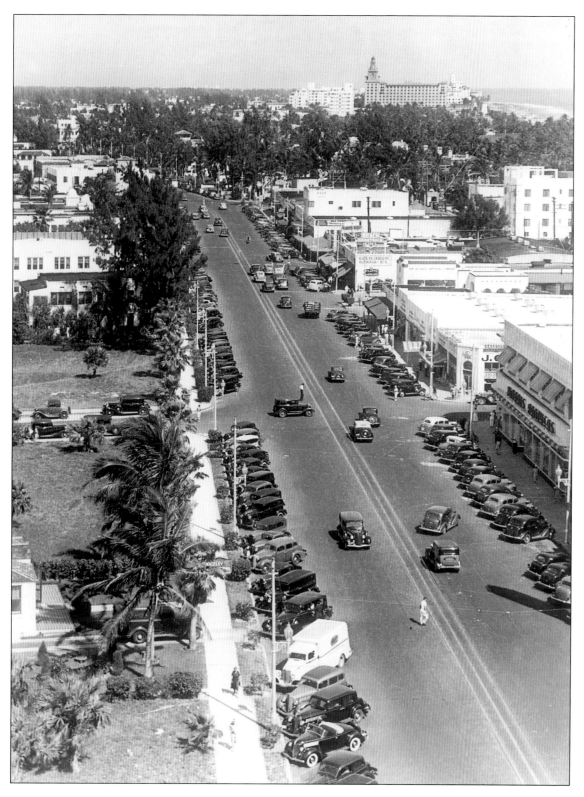

Left: This 1935 view from the City Hall tower evokes the atmosphere of a small tropical town landscaped with palms and Australian pines. Washington Avenue, two blocks west of the ocean, is Miami Beach's main commercial street and was once the trolley route to Miami. In the distance, the Roney Plaza Hotel with its Spanish Baroque tower, designed by Schultze and Weaver, dominates the skyline.

Right: Washington Avenue has undergone many changes. The drumlike building (center left) at the corner of Thirteenth Street is the 1937 Art Deco style post office. Although the old Roney Plaza was demolished in 1968, the round pyramidal turret of the Loews Miami Beach Hotel (top right), designed by John Nichols and completed in 1999, serves as a new local landmark. The yellow-topped building to its right is the 2002 Arquitectonica-designed Royal Palm Crowne Plaza Resort.

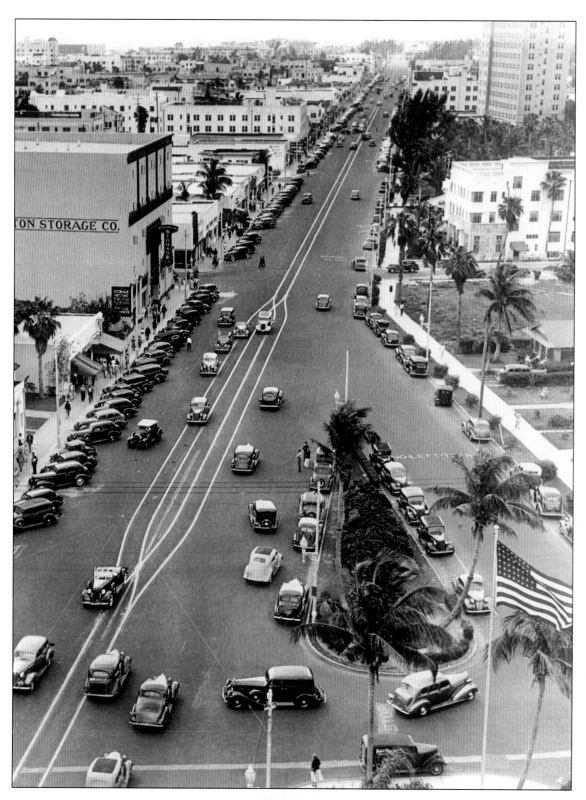

Drexel Avenue is at lower right in this c. 1940 view. The twelve-story Blackstone Hotel (top right), built in 1929, was one of the few large hotels that catered to a Jewish clientele. The white building beneath it is the Astor Hotel, built in 1936. The small coral-rock house (center right) was the home of Henri Levy, developer of Normandy Isle. The Washington Storage Company (left) opened in 1927 and expanded from three to five stories in 1936.

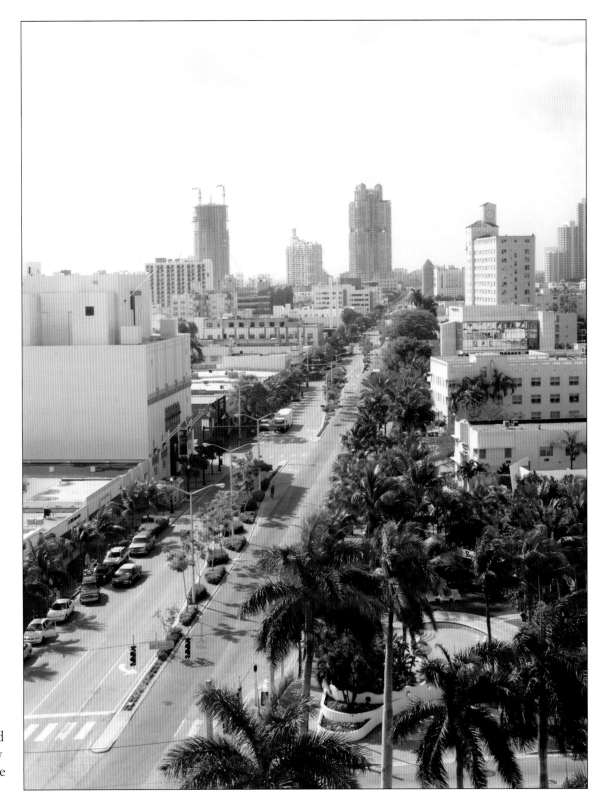

The Washington Storage Building, with two stories added in 1992, is now the Wolfsonian/Florida International University and houses the Mitchell Wolfson Jr. collection of 1885–1945 decorative arts. The Blackstone and Astor Hotels are intact. The Drexel Avenue block is now a Best Western Hotel complex, including Henri Levy's house and the Davis Hotel (center right), designed in 1941 by Henry Hohauser. The towering condominiums in the distance are at the southern tip of Miami Beach.

Much to the dismay of local residents, gangster Al Capone moved to Palm Island a few years after it was created from bay bottom. He bought a house here in 1928 and added an above-grade swimming pool and this loggia, or pool house, the following year. Although Capone was involved in local bootlegging and gambling operations, he strove to maintain a normal family life. Here, in 1930, his son hosts local children at a backyard birthday party.

When Al Capone went to prison in 1931, his family continued to reside in the Palm Island home. After his release, Capone lived out his last years here as an invalid and died in the house in 1947. The main house, two-story gatehouse, pool, and this loggia remain as a private residence and a popular attraction on sightseeing tours.

The Collins-Pancoast family had set aside some of their land for a public park even before Miami Beach was incorporated. The John S. Collins Memorial Library is seen here being dedicated in Collins Park on February 26, 1931, as the city's first public library building. Collins's own grandson, Russell T. Pancoast, designed the building. In 1937, sculptor Gustav Bohland added friezes of local scenery over the doors.

The Collins Library was rededicated as the Bass Museum of Art in 1964, housing the fine arts collection of John and Johanna Bass. The building has had several expansions, most recently Arata Isozaki's avant-garde 2001 addition (*inset*). The Collins Park neighborhood is now being revitalized. In addition to the Bass, a new building for the Miami City Ballet and a proposed regional library will complete the cultural campus.

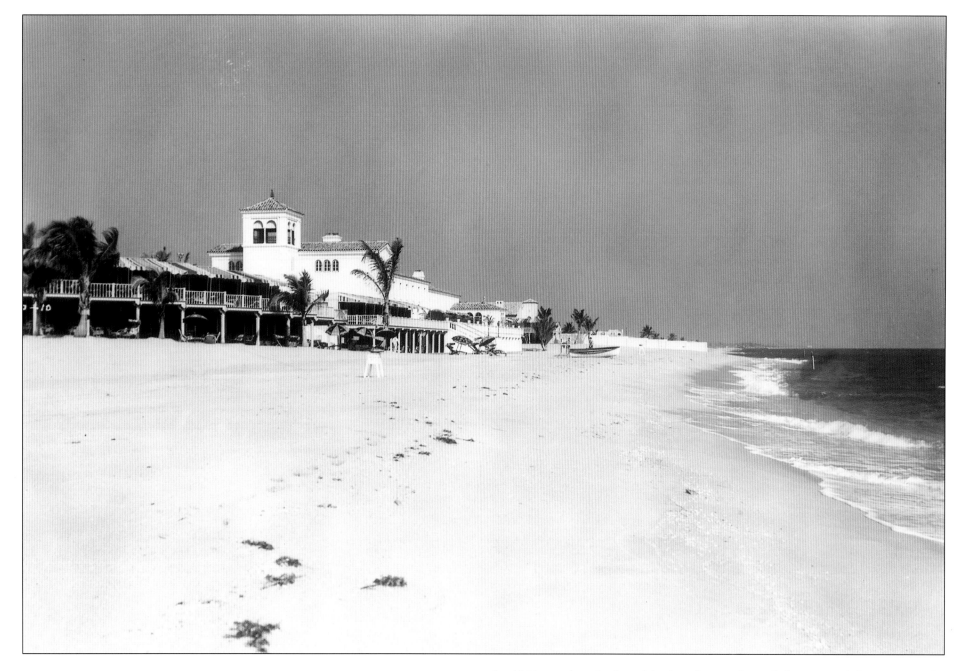

In 1930, one hundred wealthy beachgoers formed their own club at Ninetieth Street, beyond the Miami Beach city limits. Architect Russell T. Pancoast designed the elegant clubhouse that soon became a Mecca for the social set. Fearing that the City of Miami Beach would annex their domain, on May 18, 1935, Surf Club members persuaded local residents to incorporate Surfside and lent the town its first year's operating budget.

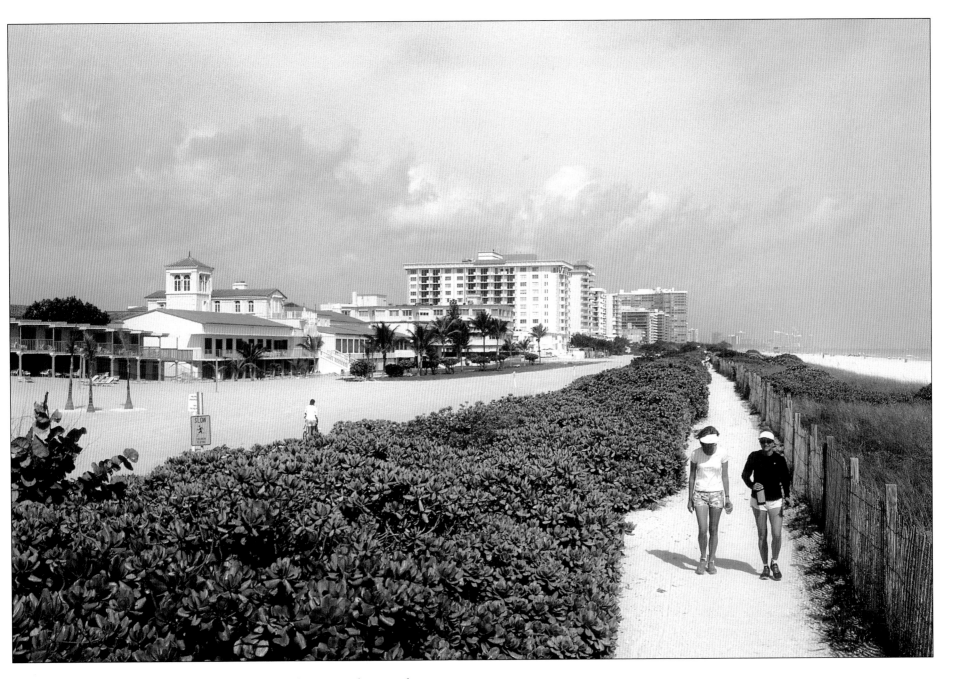

Winston Churchill stayed at the Surf Club several times and enjoyed painting by the ocean. Still an elegant private club, the original clubhouse is intact, with dining rooms, a ballroom, a pool, cabanas, and twenty-six hotel rooms open only to the Surf Club's 350 members and their guests. Surfside remains a low-rise residential neighborhood, with the taller buildings of Bal Harbour beyond.

12-16-39
X14980

P. J. DAVIS Building Construction

Left: A symphony of horizontal and vertical elements, with its curved, ribbed corner and towering neon-sign pylon, the 1939 Tiffany Hotel is a masterpiece of tropical Art Deco designed by Miami Beach's master architect L. Murray Dixon. The futuristic architecture of the 1939 New York World's Fair clearly influenced its design. Soon after its completion, it became one of the hundreds of "barracks hotels" for World War II trainees.

Right: Today this beautifully restored building is a gem in the historic district. But the Tiffany has lost its name. When the famous jewelry company sued the hotel for trademark "dilution," local preservationists lobbied Congress to pass legislation in November 1999 that protects any designated historic property from such lawsuits. But it was too late for the Tiffany. The pylon still stands, but the hotel now does business as simply "The Hotel."

Miami Beach's revolutionary Art Deco architecture used simple geometrical shapes and common building materials in imaginative ways. Here, opposite Lummus Park (right), two Art Deco style hotels, the 1939 Winter Haven (far left), designed by Albert Anis, and the 1938 Crescent (center), by Henry Hohauser, flank the more traditional Mediterranean Revival style Edgewater Beach Hotel, designed by Roy F. France in 1935. France also designed the Art Deco style St. Moritz (center) in 1939.

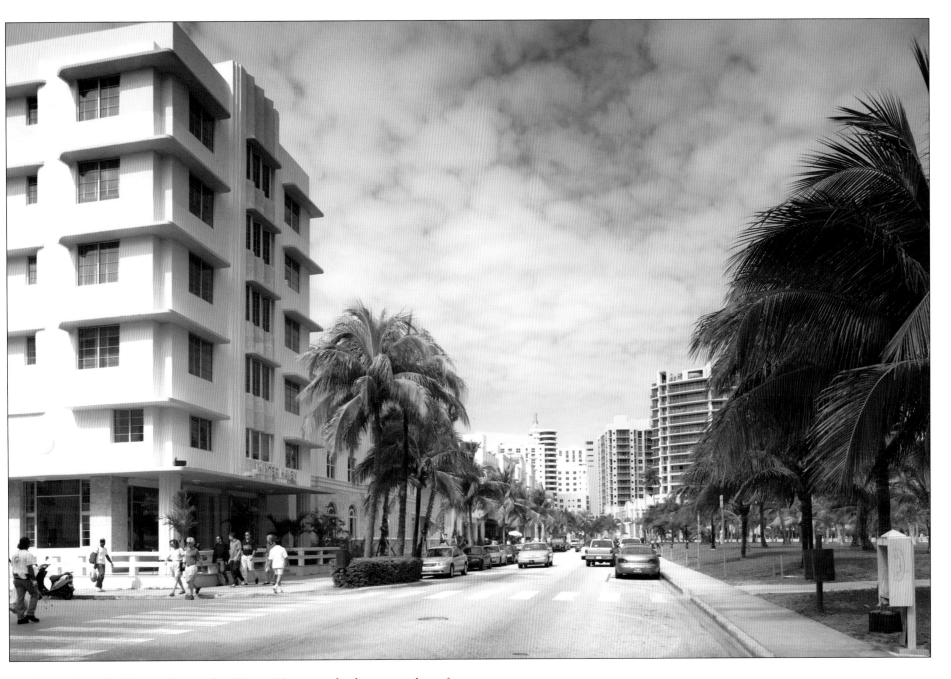

At the north end of Ocean Drive, the Winter Haven and other reminders of the irrepressible spirit of Depression-era Miami Beach line the way to an enclave of the city's newest twenty-first century architecture: Arquitectonica's Royal Palm Crowne Plaza; the Loews Miami Beach Hotel, incorporating the restored St. Moritz; Ocean Steps; Michael Graves's 1500 Ocean Drive; and Il Villaggio. This is Miami—then and now—the best of both worlds.

Nothing shows off Miami's magic better than her luminous skyline reflecting on a mirror bay. In this late 1940s view, the pinnacle of the Everglades Hotel, once Miami's finest (middle), serves as a centerpiece for the Magic City. Soon after this picture was taken, workmen turned it into a nondescript hulk when they chopped off its tower to accommodate the antennae of WTVJ, Florida's first television station.

As night falls, the Magic City comes alive, throwing jewels of many colors across the water—reflecting in the glow. From Brickell to Bayside, stately silhouettes vie with each other for attention. As the sky darkens, the city's ever-changing skyline illuminates the stage for the next Miami that waits impatiently in the wings, preparing to emerge.

INDEX